Anthropology Beyond the University

Anthropology Beyond the University

ALDEN REDFIELD, Editor

Southern Anthropological Society
Proceedings, No. 7

SOUTHERN ANTHROPOLOGICAL SOCIETY
Distributed by the University of Georgia Press
Athens 30602

SOUTHERN ANTHROPOLOGICAL SOCIETY

Founded 1966

Officers 1972-1973

E. Pendleton Banks, President

Charles M. Hudson, President Elect

Miles Richardson, Secretary-Treasurer

Arden R. King, Councilor

Wilfrid C. Bailey, Councilor

Hester A. Davis, Councilor

Irma Honigmann, Editor

Thomas K. Fitzgerald, Program Chairman

Harriet J. Kupferer, Local Arrangements Chairman

Contents

Preface

THE Southern Anthropological Society at its seventh annual meeting, February 24–26, 1972, in Columbia, Missouri, featured in its key symposium "Anthropology Beyond the University." *Proceedings No. 7* records and expands the symposium. Most of the papers presented here received their first public airing at that forum, but because we sought to sample widely the diverse fields beyond the university within which anthropologists apply their skills, we scouted other sessions and meetings for the papers by Cora S. Balmat, Carl M. Gussin, and the joint paper by C. Ronald Rosenstiel and Jeffrey B. Freeland.

I am grateful to Alden Redfield who conceived and organized the symposium and brought it to fulfillment. Special thanks go to the Museum of Anthropology and the Department of Anthropology of the University of Missouri for their efficient, gracious hosting of the 1972 meeting.

Irma Honigmann
SAS Editor

Anthropology Beyond the University

ALDEN REDFIELD

THROUGHOUT college, students are taught a series of facts and ideas, but often these are presented in such a way that the student is unable to apply them directly to his future life. Each facet of university life tends to be isolated from the next: geology may be taken but not seen in relationship to zoology, or archeology is studied but not considered as a different view of the ideas studied as history. This isolation must be compensated for by each student, who unites his training into a core of knowledge useful in earning his living later.

The field of anthropology is amazingly broad, not only with reference to its related fields, but also within its own four subdisciplines: cultural anthropology, physical anthropology, linguistics, and archeology. Each of these subdisciplines is so broad that a student can become confused trying to locate its boundaries. For example, one physical anthropologist is studying the growth and development of monkeys while another is primarily concerned with odd variations among Indian skeletons.

What are the common threads that tie these diverse fields of research together? The purpose of this book is to attempt to illustrate some of the interrelationships between anthropology and other fields, offering students the opportunity to discover inductively some of the core ideas in anthropology. Furthermore, the potential job market for people with training in anthropology, whether consisting of a few courses or a graduate degree, is indicated in a number of these fields. A Ph.D. degree may be essential for a university career in teaching anthropology, but understanding our approach to research and problems will be helpful for many who do not plan to become professionals in our discipline.

The fields included under physical anthropology stretch from the analysis of man's physical body through related aspects in primatology to equipment design for maximum adaptation to the human form. Our body is a complex mechanism, and its development over the last two million years, as well as during an individual's lifetime, forms the core of physical anthropology. Specialists study teeth, changes in bones, the shape of the skull, racial similarities or differences, and the evolution of our species. Related aspects include the study of blood types and fingerprints, the development of other primates, and the identification of bodies brought in by the police. This last feature of physical anthropology, called forensic anthropology, is usually not well known to our students.

The study of man's past as seen in the material items left behind constitutes archeology. It started with classical studies of the cultures in the Mediterranean area and the analysis of the prehistoric remains in the New World. Fields like underwater and historical archeology have developed, with special resources and training to meet special problems. The need for archeological work is increasing as our civilization destroys more and more of the sites where man has lived before. This is done both inadvertently through road and dam construction and intentionally to get "nice" things to sell or collect as a hobby. The results of archeological labor can be seen around the world in museums, tourist attractions, and in the thousands of popular books pouring onto the stands.

Under cultural anthropology is included the work of ethnologists, cultural anthropologists, and social anthropologists, all of whom study living people. Earlier generations of specialists in this field tended to focus their research on primitive groups; now we study modern man in many situations as well as the South Seas natives. Work in mental health clinics, drug rehabilitation, the schools, and other current problem areas have led cultural anthropologists to the forefront of those looking for solutions to our problems.

In the most general terms, the study of language as a concept, rather than any specific spoken language, is dealt with in the field of linguistics. Although most men in this field are employed by the universities, some work with industry in computational linguistics, others with language problems in education for the Army, Peace Corps, Bureau of Indian Affairs, and other groups dealing with multilingual situations.

As one of the newest fields in the social sciences, anthropology has not yet achieved the recognition it deserves. For example, the military has no classification for us. If you were drafted after earning an M.A. in anthropology, it would be very difficult to find a situation in which you could apply your training. At the same time, major Army and Navy laboratories are doing extensive work on clothing, body measurements, and equipment design using anthropologists. Nevertheless, recognition is growing. Many schools are now adding anthropology to their curriculums at the university, college, and even high school and elementary school levels.This has provided a number of jobs in the academic field. Every week approximately two museums are started, usually with little money and a small staff. Some hire anthropologists, although most are concerned with history or more general natural history.

For many people, the life of a teacher in an academic setting may hold little appeal; the researcher separated from teaching represents a rare individual. What other opportunities are available? A knowledge of anthropology can be applied in many areas: industrial engineering, animal research, public health services, parks and recreation, as well as in education. The papers written for this book reflect the wide-ranging influence of our discipline in the Federal Aviation Administration, National Park Service, Bureau of Indian Affairs, Smithsonian Institution, as well as through the National Institute of Mental Health and state archeological programs. Written by knowledgeable people in each field, they represent the active side of anthropology; these men have left the ivory tower of the university for the confusion of the everyday world. As the director of a university museum, I have a foot in each camp, as do several of the authors. All of us, however, are doing our active research beyond the walls of the university.

Forensic Anthropology

CLYDE C. SNOW

FORENSIC anthropology encompasses the application of the physical anthropologist's specialized knowledge of human sexual, racial, age, and individual variation to problems of medical jurisprudence. This definition includes the occasional cases in which the physical anthropologist is asked to render an expert opinion on the racial background of an adopted child or to offer testimony on the genetic constitution of parties involved in disputed paternity proceedings (Schwidetzky 1954). However, the most frequent type of case is that involving the identification of unknown skeletal remains for law enforcement agencies.

Aside from the humanitarian reason of relieving the anxiety of the next-of-kin, there are a number of very practical reasons for establishing the positive identification of the dead. While there is much variation from country to country and, within the United States, from state to state, the law generally requires that a body be identified before a death certificate can be issued. Until that time, the person is considered legally alive no matter how convincing the evidence that he is actually dead. In most countries, seven to ten years may elapse before a missing person can be legally declared dead. There are certain exceptions in the cases of mass disaster in which a missing person may be certified as dead within a shorter time if there is reasonable evidence to support the probability of death, even though no body is recovered. For example, in Sweden and Denmark the period is shortened to three years, and in Norway death may be certified immediately after the disaster (Gustafson 1966:17).

Whatever its length, the interim between actual death and its certification can be difficult for the survivors. Wills cannot be probated, claims to succession are in abatement, and property of the decedent cannot be disposed of even though it depreciates greatly in value and its maintenance works an intolerable hardship on the survivors. Many insurance companies will not make settlements until a death certificate is issued. Spouses may not remarry and, in the case of business partnerships, crucial business transactions may be paralyzed until the missing partner is officially declared dead.

Finally, positive identification of the victim is generally a necessity in criminal cases, since without the *corpus delicti*, the chances for a successful prosecution are rather slim.

The history of forensic anthropology is intertwined with the development of forensic medicine, forensic odontology, toxicology, and other areas of scientific criminology during the nineteenth century (Thorwald 1964; Camps 1968). During this period, most problems of skeletal identification were handled by the pathologists themselves by applying the osteological rules-of-thumb concerning sex, race, and age differences found in the writings and texts of early anatomists.

The fact that dentists could generally recognize their own handiwork began to be fully appreciated during this period. The earliest forensic odontologist we know of in this country was Paul Revere (Forbes 1942). Along with candlestick holders and midnight rides, Revere made dentures "of teeth and tusks of the hyppotomus or sea horse" or, in a pinch, wired unretouched sheep's teeth into the patient's mouth. Sheep's teeth were less expensive than the "hyppotomus" models, but according to Revere, "their peculiar forms were . . . a great obstacle to correct fitting" (Forbes 1942: 124). Sometime in the early 1770s, Revere set two teeth for Dr. Joseph Warren, a prominent Boston physician who was also, like Revere, a member of the radical left. Later, it was Warren, provided with information on British intentions by his extensive network of spies, who launched Revere on his famous ride.

In 1775 Warren was killed at the Battle of Bunker Hill. The victorious British buried his body with that of another American soldier in an unmarked grave (Cary 1961:222). A year later the bodies were disinterred by Warren's brother and Revere was asked to help with the identification. He was able to recognize the two teeth and the silver wire that he had used in wiring them to the adjacent natural teeth (Forbes 1942:301).

Another landmark in forensic identification occurred in Boston in 1849. This was the famous Parkman murder (Sullivan 1971) which resulted in the trial of a professor of Harvard University where, in those days, campus violence was not necessarily the exclusive prerogative of students (Birkenhead 1929:173–184).[1]

The victim, Dr. George Parkman, was a well-to-do elderly physician who had largely retired from practice to look after his investments. This latter was mostly small rental dwellings scattered throughout the poorer districts of Boston. He collected his rents personally and he had a rigidly scheduled round of collection which he accomplished on foot. He was tall and very thin, seldom smiled or spoke, and was characterized by a strongly undershot lower jaw which earned him the nickname "Chin" among the street people of Boston. He was a strict landlord but punctilious in his business dealings.

The alleged murderer, Dr. John White Webster, was a professor of chemistry at Harvard. He was considered an able chemist but a poor lecturer. Briefly, his problem was this: he had a wife, three unmarried daughters, expensive tastes, and an annual income of about nineteen hundred dollars. Between 1842 and 1847, Webster borrowed several thousand dollars from Parkman. In 1848, needing more money and afraid to return to Parkman, he borrowed twelve hundred dollars from a third party, using a mineral collection already mortgaged to Parkman as security. When informed of Webster's shoddy dealings, Parkman became infuriated and demanded instant repayment, threatening public exposure. This harassment continued for several weeks, with Parkman berating Webster whenever they met in public.

It is possible that the breaking point occurred when Dr. Parkman began attending Webster's lectures, occupying a front-row seat and glaring at him in silent contempt. Any of us who become easily rattled during lectures can well understand that by such behavior Dr. Parkman may have signed his own death warrant.

Harassed beyond endurance, Webster invited Parkman to his laboratory in the medical school under the pretext of making a settlement. According to Webster, Dr. Parkman arrived punctually at 1:30 P.M. on November 23, 1848. Webster said that he made a payment on the note which satisfied Parkman and the latter left the laboratory shortly before 2:00 P.M. Parkman did not return home for supper, and his family instituted a widespread search which soon centered on the medical school, the last place he was known to have visited. The premises, including Dr. Webster's laboratory, were searched by the police, but no trace of Dr. Parkman was found.

However, the school janitor, Ephraim Littlefield, had become suspicious of the professor and, being an inveterate snoop, spent most of the succeeding week poking around the premises and spying on Webster. Apparently one of the Harvard faculty status symbols of those days was a private privy. At any rate, Dr. Webster's laboratory was provided with such a convenience, which he kept locked to prevent its defilement by such academic riffraff as laboratory assistants and graduate students. For some reason, the privy was not inspected in the police search—probably because the officers, while able to entertain the hypothesis that one Harvard alumnus might conceivably stoop to murder another, could not imagine his being so ungentlemanly as to hide the body in a privy. However, no man is a hero to his janitor and Littlefield was not put off by such snobbish presumptions. Possessed with an energy seldom observed in an academic building custodian, he spent most of the Thanksgiving holiday, November 29, as well as the next day boring through the five-course brick wall that separated the privy vault from the sub-basement. When he finally broke through, he found a disarticulated human pelvis, a right thigh, and left lower leg. The ungrateful wretch, who only the day before had feasted on a seven-pound Thanksgiving turkey given him by Webster, informed the police, thereby cooking the professor's goose along with his turkey.

When the police returned, they found other items overlooked in the first search, including an eviscerated human thorax and a left thigh concealed in a metal tea chest and some charred fragments of human bone in a laboratory furnace. Most damning of all were the remains of some false teeth (Wentworth and Wilder 1932:91).

A committee of medical experts, made up almost entirely of Webster's colleagues at the Harvard Medical School, convened to examine the remains. Dr. Jeffries Wyman, Hersey professor of anatomy, made a most detailed study of the bones and gave the central testimony regarding them at the subsequent trial. From their examination, Webster's colleagues were able to state that the remains were human, the various parts were from the same body, and that they had been dismembered by someone with a limited knowledge of anatomy. (Webster had last dissected a cadaver in medical school some twenty-five years previously.) The parts contained no residue of chemicals used at the school to preserve the dissection cadavers. Age was assessed at fifty to sixty years and, from the long bones, stature was estimated at 5 feet 10½ inches; Dr. Parkman was sixty years old at the time of his disappearance and was 5 feet 11 inches tall (Polson 1955:96).

Helping Dr. Wyman in his initial examination and, later, also testifying as a medical expert for the prosecution, was Dr. Oliver Wendell Holmes, the "Autocrat at the Breakfast Table" and the father of the future chief justice of the United States Supreme Court. At this time Holmes was dean of the Harvard Medical School as well as Parkman professor of anatomy. This latter chair had been named in honor of the victim when, several years previously, he had donated the land on which the Medical School was built.

When the building was completed, a dedication ceremony had been held at which Dr. Parkman had been one of the guests of honor. Wishing to appear at his best for this occasion, Parkman had asked his dentist, Dr. Nathan Keep—who later became dean of the Harvard Dental School—to prepare him a set of dentures. He requested them shortly before the dedication ceremony and, characteristically, told Dr. Keep that if he couldn't complete the dentures in time, he wouldn't accept them at all. Dr. Keep undertook the task and barely beat the deadline. So pressed was he that he had to do some last-minute grinding on the mandibular denture which left some peculiar marks that he was able to identify. In the course of his work he had made an impression of Dr. Parkman's peculiar lower jaw and, fortunately, had retained the model. The denture fragments from the furnace, when reassembled, fit the model perfectly and the peculiar grinding marks were still visible.

The Parkman case is interesting because the rationale used in examining the remains was essentially the same as that employed in such cases today. It may best be outlined as a series of questions: Are the remains human? If human, do they represent a single individual or the commingled remains of several? Are they recent enough to be of forensic interest (less than fifty to seventy-five years old)? What is the individual's age? sex? race? stature? Do they display any signs of disease, anomalies, or physical peculiarities that might help to establish identification? Do they display signs of violence that may indicate the manner of death?

In the Parkman case, the central problem was that of determining the identity of a single individual. At the other extreme are mass disasters in which positive identification must be established for dozens or sometimes hundreds of individuals. In aircraft crashes, particularly, positive identification is important since it is an essential step in the scientific investigation of the accident.

Such investigations, in air and other transportation accidents, are carried out by the National Transportation Safety Board (NTSB) with two objectives (Leak 1968). The first objective is to establish, if possible, the probable cause of the accident. Naturally, determination of probable cause is of great importance because it may provide knowledge enabling us to prevent such accidents in the future. As embodied in the official NTSB report on the accident, it is also the prime source document on which litigation growing out of the accident is based. A second objective is to provide the Federal Aviation Administration, airlines, and manufacturers with information on human factors which, while perhaps not preventing future accidents, can lead to greater protection for the passengers and crew—in other words, to increase their survivability (Snow et al. 1970).

Scattered within the wreckage of a passenger aircraft are the bodies of its victims. To the inexperienced eye, the distribution of the bodies may appear as haphazard as the rubble itself. To human factors investigators, however, each body has a tale to tell which, when related to structural evidence, can lead to a reconstruction of the crash and post-crash events (Reals 1968). The first step in reconstruction occurs on the scene which is carefully mapped. Such maps include the exact location of each body and its relation to surrounding structural debris. Usually unidentified at this stage, each body is tagged with a number before removal from the wreckage.

When the bodies are removed to the morgue, the identification process is initiated. Fingerprints are taken if possible, and dental charts are made to be compared with those of passengers whose names appear on the manifest (Luntz and Luntz 1972). Personal effects, such as wallets, rings, and wrist watches, found with the body are catalogued, as are labels and laundry marks on the victim's clothing. Afterward, the forensic pathologists begin their work, keeping a close watch for autopsy evidence that may be useful in identification, such as anomalies, old operation scars, surgically removed organs, and signs of chronic disease. More important, the autopsy pathologists seek to provide a detailed inventory of all signs of accident trauma from the smallest burns and scratches to the major, lethal injuries.

Concurrent with these activities in the morgue, the crash survivors (if any) are also being examined. Detailed abstracts of all their injuries are obtained from hospital records, and as soon as they feel up to it, they are interviewed extensively by trained accident investigators. During these interviews, survivors are asked to recall every possible detail, no matter how insignificant, from the time they boarded the aircraft until they made their escape.

Meanwhile, at the accident scene, other investigators are sifting through the wreckage to document the structural damage to the cabin interior. They pay particular attention to seats and seat belts, to see if there is evidence of tie-down failure and, if so, in which direction failure occurred. The condition of emergency exits, escape slides, emergency lighting systems, and other safety devices is examined for evidence of malfunction. They also make detailed notes or maps of the location of items of personal possession such as coats, hats, briefcases, and purses that passengers leave behind during escape.

Eventually, by relating body location, survivor accounts, and structural evidence, a picture emerges which allows an accurate reconstruction of the immediate pre- and post-accident events. Usually, for example, it is possible to determine the seating arrangement of passengers at the time of the accident. When this is related to the exits used by the survivors and the body locations of the victims, the evacuation pattern is determined. Study of this pattern helps pinpoint environmental factors such as post-crash debris, poor exit lighting, and faulty crew procedures which may have impeded escape. The extent and types of injuries to both survivors and fatalities are also studied and sometimes help us isolate structural deficiencies which can be remedied by improved design (Hasbrook 1958; Swearingen 1971).

To illustrate the role of identification in determining the cause of an aircraft accident, I can think of no better example than the crash of a National Airlines DC–6B which occurred in North Carolina during the early morning hours of January 6, 1960 (Doyle 1968). The flight, National 2511, departed from New York close to midnight. After a routine position check at 2:33 A.M. over Wilmington, North Carolina, there was no further contact with the plane, and it was presumed missing. The next day it was found crashed on a farm near Bolivia, North Carolina.

With the aid of ground witnesses, the probable flight of the aircraft was reconstructed. From the Wilmington checkpoint, it had continued a southward course, skirting the Atlantic coast slightly inland and over the Cape Fear River. Along this path, in an area called Snow's Marsh, some debris of the aircraft was found. This point was about sixteen miles east of the main crash site at Bolivia. It was surmised that the flight was normal until the aircraft was over the Snow's Marsh area where the debris was located. At this point, something happened to account for the sudden right turn inland toward the crash site at Bolivia. Whether the turn was executed by the captain in an attempt to return to Wilmington or because the aircraft was out of control could not be determined.

At departure there were twenty-nine passengers and five crew aboard the airplane. Only thirty-three bodies were found at the crash site. Autopsies led to the identification of the thirty-three victims. The missing body was that of Julian Andrew Frank, a passenger from New York City.

Meanwhile, investigators began the tedious task of reassembling the wreckage. The reconstruction revealed a large hole in the right side of the fuselage adjacent to the leading edge of the wing. Many of the pieces of debris found at the Snow's Marsh site came from the vicinity of the hole in the aircraft. Analysis of the mock-up by engineers ruled out possible causes such as structural failure or rapid cabin decompression. Interest then centered on an explosion as the possible cause of the crash. Unfortunately, no trace of nitrate deposits—the usual residue of explosives—could be found, but by this time the wreckage had been exposed for several days in rainy weather, and nitrates are water soluble.

A few days after the crash, a body was found in Snow's Marsh. Although badly mutilated, an autopsy revealed it to be that of Julian Frank, the missing passenger. Both legs of the body were missing and, according to the ballistic experts, the injuries resembled those seen in soldiers who have stepped on land mines. The autopsy pathologist noted that the injuries to some of Frank's remaining fingers indicated exposure to a high explosive force. Embedded in an aircraft life jacket found in the Snow's Marsh debris was a zipper tooth and blue threads similar to those of carry-on flight bags. Also in Snow's Marsh were the remnants of a three-seat unit from the vicinity of the hole in the aircraft. The forward edge of one seat cover had been shredded in a manner similar to Frank's legs. Around the seat and in adjacent structures, nitrates were detected along with scattered residues of manganese dioxide. The latter substance is used in dry-cell batteries—a common component of homemade bombs. Bits of wire not belonging to any structure of the aircraft were also discovered. In the vicinity of the seat, some human tissue was found embedded in one of the ventilating units. Examination revealed that it also contained traces of nitrate. Embedded in the flesh of Frank's lower torso were numerous pieces of wire and metal debris.

Finally, approximately two months after the accident, the last piece of the grisly jigsaw was discovered. A 26-cm. fragment from the distal end of a human left fibula was found lodged in an overhead hat rack in the main fuselage near the site of the explosion. Adhering to it were cloth fragments matching the remnants of trousers found on Frank's body. Embedded in the tissues attached to the bone was a brace retainer plate from a Westclox "Travette" alarm clock. In the CAB report on this accident (Civil Aeronautics Board 1960), it was concluded that

> at approximately 0233 a dynamite charge was exploded, initiated by means of a dry-cell battery within the passenger cabin and at a point beneath the extreme right seat of seat row No. 7.
>
> Mr. Julian A. Frank was in close proximity to the dynamite charge when the detonation occurred. (P. 7)

The FBI found that Mr. Frank had insured himself for approximately one and a quarter million dollars shortly before the flight (Doyle 1968).

In the century between Dr. Parkman's murder and the mid-air explosion over Snow's Marsh, murderers have become no less ingenious in disposing of their victims' bodies, and mass disasters, if anything, seem larger and more frequent. Therefore, the need for more rapid and more reliable methods of identification of the dead is pressing. The contribution of physical anthropology to this problem can be considered in terms of research, training, and active participation in the field.

In terms of research, physical anthropologists have directed comparatively little effort to forensic problems. Nevertheless, nearly every physical anthropological study and especially those dealing with the human skeletal variation and paleopathology can, at times, be applied to specific problems in human identification. For example, sometimes we encounter a skeleton with a disease or deformity which might be useful in personal identification. Recognition and diagnosis of such a feature grossly from the dry bone is difficult for the pathologist who usually makes his diagnosis microscopically from fresh tissues and even for the radiologist who spends most of his time viewing x-rays and seldom sees a real bone. To classify such pathologies accurately, they must often turn to the paleopathological literature in which physical anthropologists and interested physicians have provided precise descriptions of the same lesions in skeletal populations perhaps thousands of years old. Our limited ability to diagnose racially the skulls of recent homicide victims comes not from research directed specifically to the problem from a forensic standpoint but is a distillate of literally hundreds of classical studies of racial variation in the human skeleton—studies undertaken by physical anthropologists to shed light on man's past. To estimate the age of a child's skeleton, we turn to the studies of Garn or Krogman and their students or to the magnificent atlases of Greulich and Pyle, whose purpose is to describe the phenomena of human growth itself and not to provide data of occasional use in identification. In this broad sense, almost all physical anthropologists may be considered contributors to the subdiscipline of forensic anthropology.

This is not entirely a one-way proposition. The small number of physical anthropologists who have directed efforts toward human identification problems have provided knowledge useful to a better understanding of human biological history. Thus studies of American World War II and Korean War dead undertaken for identification purposes have led to the studies by Trotter (Trotter and Gleser 1952, 1958; Trotter 1970) on the prediction of stature from skeletal remains and by McKern and Stewart (1957) on variability in ossification events in late adolescence and early maturity. Trotter's statural prediction equations are basic to studies of stature increase in prehistoric populations such as that by Huber (1968). McKern and Stewart's data on skeletal aging allow paleodemographers to more accurately reconstruct mortality curves for skeletal populations (Brothwell 1971).

In a recent review of progress in forensic anthropology, Stewart (1972) points out that the thrust of research in this area during the past few decades has been toward the statistical honing of our various assessments and estimates that we routinely make in the identification of an individual skeleton.

Thus many years ago anatomists might have said that a pelvis was probably female because the pubis was "long" and the sciatic notch "wide." Just how long was "long" and how wide was "wide" was a matter of subjective judgment which was sometimes confounded by lack of appreciation of the normal range of overlap between the sexes. A long step forward was made by Schultz (1930) who quantified sexual difference in the relative length of the pubis by defining the *ischiopubic index* and provided some rather precise and useful data on its sexual variation in different races. A few years later Hanna and Washburn (1953) devised a technique for accurately measuring the angle of the sciatic notch and, by relating this feature to the ischiopubic index, found that they could correctly assess sex of unknown skeletons with about 95 percent confidence. With an experienced eye and a little luck, the old-time expert was probably right about as often as we are today. His problem was that he hadn't the haziest notion of his chances of being wrong. Nowadays, using the knowledge provided by Hanna and Washburn, or the even more elegant discriminant function techniques of Thieme and Schull (1957), Giles and Elliott (1963), and Howells (1970), we can sex a skeleton more confidently but, even more important, assign a rather precise probability to our chance of being right (or wrong). Chance is a matter of at least mild importance, shall we say, to a defendant who might be hanged on the basis of a misidentified skeleton.

This progress toward greater precision in our estimates applies not only to sexual assessments but also to our racial diagnoses and our estimates of age and stature. The general trend of research has been to replace dogma based on the mean with a healthy scepticism based on the standard deviation.

Training in forensic anthropology has been slow and spotty. I know of only about half a dozen departments that offer formal courses in this subject. Usually a lecture and a lab session on skeletal identification squeezed in at the end of the semester are about all that the student encounters. This is unfortunate because, as those of us who go into this area soon realize, there are a number of problems beyond the simple manipulation of the bones with which we must deal. To give a specific example, we can return again to that small but frustrating percentage of skeletons of whose sex we can never be quite certain. Usually these will display a few small features and traits which suggest a diagnosis of male or female—even though we realize that in a large number of such instances such "guesstimates" are likely to be wrong. If the population we are studying consists of several hundred skeletons, it is easier and perfectly permissible to indulge our intuitions and assign such doubtful cases to one sex or the other since, in the long run, the errors will tend to cancel each other out. In a forensic case, such a misclassification is apt to be very misleading and eventually embarrassing; so it is best when confronted with one of these ambiguous skeletons to face the situation boldly, tell the police that you cannot be sure whether the individual was a man or a woman, and suggest that they best search their files for missing persons of both sexes. This might temporarily tarnish your image with the local police, but it will not destroy it entirely as would be the case if the petite skeleton you diagnose as female turns out to be a missing male hairdresser or somebody like that. Of course, if you are verbally adroit, you can actually enhance your local reputation by cloaking your indecision with a scholarly phrase. For this I recommend the Latin term *incertae sedis*, which I found in an old taxonomy text. Neither I nor the Oklahoma police are quite sure what it means, but it is infinitely more elegant than "pussy-foot."

This is merely one of a number of problems you will encounter in forensic work. Others involve more serious dealings with the police, the press, and sometimes, if you are asked to testify as an expert, with lawyers, judges, and court procedures. More time should be devoted to these and other special problems in our graduate student training of physical anthropologists.

In 1971, thanks largely to the efforts of Dr. Ellis Kerley of the University of Maryland, the American Academy of Forensic Science has given formal recognition to a new subdiscipline by establishing a Forensic Anthropology Section. To date we have recruited about twenty-five members—all physical anthropologists who have experience or research interests in human identification. It is hoped that this development will serve to attract students and stimulate research in a hitherto neglected but exciting field.

Now let us return to Professor Webster, whom we left dangling (almost literally) in suspense, awaiting the jury's verdict. He was found guilty and, since in those days academic tenure offered no protection against capital punishment, he was hanged on August 29, 1851. It should be noted that in the years since much evidence in favor of his innocence has been discovered which was not brought out at his trial. Some legal scholars build a strong case against the janitor, Ephraim Littlefield, who, they believe, robbed and murdered Dr. Parkman after he left Professor Webster and then planted the remains in his laboratory. Since the defendant; the victims; the four justices of the court; all the lawyers, both for the prosecution and for the defense; all the medical experts; and most of the witnesses were Harvard graduates or faculty members, we would have to suppose that, if Webster were innocent, the best legal and scientific minds of that great university were bamboozled by a barely literate janitor. Of course, for this very same reason, Yale alumni maintain that Littlefield was probably the murderer.

NOTE

1. I åm grateful to Lester L. Luntz, D.D.S., of Hartford, Connecticut, for awakening my interest in the Parkman case. Dr. Luntz, a scholar of forensic odontology and a fellow "Parkmaniac," has in the course of his studies of Dr. Keep's original dental impressions discovered much new material on the circumstances surrounding Dr. Parkman's murder.

REFERENCES

Birkenhead, Fredrick Edwin Smith, 1st Earl, 1929. *More Famous Trials* (Garden City, N.Y.: Doubleday, Doran), pp. 178–184.

Brothwell, Don R., 1971. Palaeodemography. In *Biological Aspects of Demography*, W. Brass, ed. (London: Taylor and Francis), pp. 111–130.

Camps, Francis E., 1968. *Gradwohl's Legal Medicine*, 2nd ed. (Bristol: John Wright and Sons).

Cary, John, 1961. *Joseph Warren, Physician, Politician, Patriot* (Urbana: University of Illinois Press).

Civil Aeronautics Board, 1960. Aircraft Accident Report: National Airlines Inc., Douglas DC–6B, N 8225H, Near Bolivia, North Carolina, January 6, 1960. File No. 1–0002 (Washington, D.C.: Civil Aeronautics Board).

Doyle, Bernard C., 1968. Aeromedical Investigations of Civil Aircraft Accidents. In *Medical Investigation of Aviation Accidents*, William J. Reals, ed. (Chicago: College of American Pathologists), pp. 38–58.

Forbes, Esther, 1942. *Paul Revere and the World He Lived In* (Boston: Houghton Mifflin).

Giles, Eugene, and Orville Elliott, 1963. Sex Determination by Discriminant Function. *American Journal of Physical Anthropology* 21:53–68.

Gustafson, Gosta, 1966. *Forensic Odontology* (New York: American Elsevier).

Hanna, R. E., and S. L. Washburn, 1953. The Determination of the Sex of Skeletons, as Illustrated by a Study of the Eskimo Pelvis. *Human Biology* 25:21–27.

Hasbrook, A. H., 1958. *Gross Pattern of Injury of 109 Survivors of Five Transport Accidents*. Cornell University, Aviation Crash Injury Research Reports, AVCIR–5–SS–96 (Ithaca, N.Y.).

Howells, W. W., 1970. Multivariate Analysis for the Identification of Race from Crania. In *Personal Identification in Mass Disasters*, T. D. Stewart, ed. (Washington, D.C.: National Museum of Natural History), pp. 111–121.

Huber, Neil M., 1968. The Problem of Stature Increase: Looking from the Past to the Present. In *The Skeletal Biology of Earlier Human Populations*, D. R. Brothwell, ed. (Oxford: Pergamon Press), pp. 67–102.

Leak, John S., 1968. Aircraft Accident Investigation: Organization and Procedures of the National Transportation Safety Board. In *Medical Investigation of Aviation Accidents*, William J. Reals, ed. (Chicago: College of American Pathologists), pp. 110–130.

Luntz, Lester L., and Phyllys Luntz, 1972. Dental Identification of Disaster Victims by a Dental Disaster Squad. *Journal of Forensic Sciences* 17:63–69.

McKern, T. W., and T. D. Stewart, 1957. *Skeletal Age Changes in Young American Males.* Quartermaster Research and Development Command, Environmental Protection Research Division, Technical Report EP–45 (Natick, Mass.)

Polson, Cyril John, 1955. *The Essentials of Forensic Medicine* (Springfield, Ill.: Charles C. Thomas).

Reals, William J., ed., 1968. *Medical Investigation of Aviation Accidents* (Chicago: College of American Pathologists).

Schultz, A. H., 1930. The Skeleton of the Trunk and Limbs of Higher Primates. *Human Biology* 2:303–438.

Schwidetzky, Ilse, 1954. Forensic Anthropology in Germany. *Human Biology* 26:1–20.

Snow, Clyde C., et al., 1970. *Survival in Emergency Escape from Passenger Aircraft.* Federal Aviation Administration, Office of Aviation Medicine Report No. FAA–AM–70–16 (Washington, D.C.).

Stewart, T. D., 1972. What the Bones Tell—Today. *FBI Law Enforcement Bulletin* 41(2):16–20.

Sullivan, Robert J., 1971. *The Disappearance of Dr. Parkman* (Boston: Little Brown).

Swearingen, John J., 1971. *General Aviation Structures Directly Responsible for Trauma in Crash Decelerations.* Federal Aviation Administration, Office of Aviation Medicine Report No. FAA–AM–71–3 (Washington, D.C.).

Thieme, Fred P., and William Schull, 1957. Sex Determination from the Skeleton. *Human Biology* 29:242–273.

Thorwald, Jurgen, 1964. *The Century of the Detective* (New York: Harcourt, Brace and World).

Trotter, Mildred, 1970. Estimation of Stature from Intact Long Limb Bones. In *Personal Identification in Mass Disasters*, T. D. Stewart, ed. (Washington, D.C.: National Museum of Natural History), pp. 71–83.

Trotter, M., and G. C. Gleser, 1952. Estimation of Stature from the Long Bones of American Whites and Negroes. *American Journal of Physical Anthropology* 10:463.

———, 1958. A Re-evaluation of Estimation of Stature Based on Measurements of Stature Taken During Life and Long Bones after Death. *American Journal of Physical Anthropology* 16:79.

Wentworth, Bert, and Harris Hawthorne Wilder, 1932. *Personal Identification: Methods for the Identification of Individuals, Living or Dead*, 2nd ed. (Chicago: T. G. Cooke).

The Physical Anthropologist in Primate Research Facilities in Africa

WILLIAM R. MAPLES

PRIMATE studies have many varied aspects. Some are conducted to understand more about the nonhuman primates. Others use the nonhuman primate as a hazy, imperfect mirror by which to view man as he was millions of years ago. Some scientists, particularly in the biomedical fields, use the nonhuman primate as a stand-in for man to test drugs, surgical techniques, and transplants before applying the procedures to humans. The variety and amount of research using nonhuman primates are staggering. Although much of the research is done in the laboratory or under other captive conditions in the United States, Europe, and Asia, much is also conducted in or near the natural habitats of the nonhuman primates. I wish to discuss the latter research, using Kenya, East Africa, as the main focus.

Most primate field investigations are carried out by one or more persons connected with universities. Very often the person is a student doing dissertation research. He has probably never been to the field, and he may be supervised by a professor who has not been to that particular place. The investigator must first locate the areas where the desired species occurs, then select the best study area, frequently losing several months in the initial stages of selecting the study population. Game parks and reserves are usually selected, often because of ease of observation and convenient facilities. It is now being recognized that protected areas are not the best choices in many cases.

Biomedical researchers seldom venture to the field without local help. Since these investigators usually require closer contact with their subjects than researchers studying behavior, local assistance is essential for shooting or trapping the study animals. Professional hunters or trappers are selected for the task, the professional hunter normally being the better choice. However, expertise in hunting trophy animals is not closely correlated with a knowledge of primate distribution and behavior nor with other skills required to hunt or trap nonhuman primates successfully. There is also a marked tendency for the investigator to become interested in helping the hunter secure "meat for the pot," with resulting neglect of the scientific investigation.

The primate study center can solve the various problems mentioned above. It can provide assistance to virtually all primate investigators, those in the field and those back in the laboratories. To be sure, primate facilities differ in their objectives and capabilities. Some limit themselves to primate conservation combined with some behavioral studies. Others concentrate their efforts in the biomedical field to such an extent that they become only trapping units. The ideal primate field center should combine all of these objectives.

For over three years, I served as manager of the Southwest Primate Research Center in Nairobi, Kenya. It is the East African branch of the Southwest Foundation for Research and Education, a biomedical research group in San Antonio, Texas. The university background acquired in physical anthropology benefited me considerably in that context. As a specialist in primatology, I received the usual general background in cultural and physical anthropology plus specialized training in primate anatomy, taxonomy, evolution, physiology, and ethology. At one time or another, practically all of this training proved useful to me. I hope that this paper will demonstrate how the almost unique blend of biological science and social science that constitutes physical anthropology gives the best foundation for an employee in a major primate field station. Perhaps I am giving one example to answer the question continually asked by prospective anthropology majors, "Yes I know what physical anthropology is, but what can you do with it besides teach?"

The Southwest Primate Research Center, when established by the Southwest Foundation, was charged with several functions, but the most important was to trap animals for use at the foundation in San Antonio. By having its own East African trapping unit, the researchers in San Antonio were assured of animals carefully selected according to age, sex, physical condition, subspecies, location, and even troop. Ecological information could be evaluated when necessary. After capture, the animals could be prepared before shipping by special diets, yellow fever vaccine, blood tests before and after immunization, tuberculosis tests, vermifuge treatment for the removal of intestinal parasites, and other kinds of specialized treatment. Careful records could be maintained on each animal from capture to shipment to the United States. The trapping function became increasingly important as the primate facility matured.

The manager of the primate center also had the responsibility of carrying out resident research projects directed by scientists in the United States. These projects usually required field samples, such as blood or bacterial swabs, to be obtained at trapping sites, or animals to be maintained in captive conditions at the primate center for long-term studies. The manager was also responsible for negotiating with the Kenya government for the capture permits and other licenses, for the use of laboratory facilities, and in other areas of cooperation. And, as a final function, the primate center furnished visiting scientists with assistance, providing them with technical advice, knowledge of local conditions, laboratory facilities, and equipment. It is in the expansion of services to visiting scientists that primate centers in East Africa could become truly important.

Despite my academic background, my training was obviously incomplete. For instance, I discovered the strength of baboons one day as I tried to immobilize one with a drug. I observed how the animals would reach through the mesh of the trap and attempt to grab the trapper. I first practiced on some weanlings and found that, when they reached for me, it was simple to grasp their arms and inject a drug (phencyclidine hydrochloride) into their arms with a hand syringe. When I tried it on a large male, I leaned away from the trap since I expected some strength on the part of the baboon, but only when I bounced on the side of the trap did the true strength of an adult male baboon become a reality for me.

Trapping nonhuman primates is probably the best example of an activity in which detailed knowledge of primate behavior brings practical results. Reciprocally, observations in the trapping area add to the pool of knowledge about primate behavior.

Water probably provides the key to trapping baboons. Baboons drink once or twice a day except in rather specialized circumstances when they obtain fluids from fruits, such as the cashew fruit. Thus, while the troop may move in many different directions within its home range during a period of a week or more, it will almost invariably come to the water source daily. Since most of East Africa is arid, water sources tend to be so distantly scattered that a troop will return to the same one each day. Indeed, several troops may use the same water source. This is the best location to place the traps. Trapping does not begin with the placement of traps, however. First, one prepares the area where the traps will be placed by scattering food, usually loose kernels of maize. In three or four days, the troop begins to depend upon this rich food supply near the water source. Troop movement becomes reduced as the animals stay in the area of food and water. Then the traps are moved in, but the doors are fixed in an open position, and feeding continues. Food is still scattered about the area, but concentrated amounts are placed near the open doors and within the traps. The baboons learn that they can go in and out of the traps with impunity. If traps had been set to close immediately, only a few bold animals would have ventured in at first and been trapped, frightening away the remainder of the troop. Once the troop has gained complete confidence in the traps, trapping can be initiated. Since as soon as the troop arrives the more dominant animals go to the concentrated food supplies in the traps, they are the first to be trapped. Once they have been removed, the troop is more likely to return again and again until almost the entire troop is trapped. A sufficient number of traps must be used to capture most of the dominant animals on the first day or so.

Sometimes it is necessary to adjust the trapping procedure somewhat. It may be more effective to use some local food item as bait rather than maize, or the trapper may find that the baboons are partially aware of how the trap functions. For example, I once had to trap a subadult, female baboon who had been previously trapped. I had no difficulty getting her to eat the scattered maize in and around the trap, but she avoided the maize cob that would release the door. She would ignore the trigger bait, leave the trap, and then add insult to injury by pulling the door down from the outside while I watched helplessly. I eventually trapped her by adding a second trigger bait placed on the floor of the trap far from the rejected dummy bait.

In the course of trapping operations, one learns a great deal about baboon behavior. One example concerns dominance. For a week, a baboon troop was observed in a trapping area before the traps were set. During this period, the dominance of the adult males was noted. They used eyelid threats, yawns, and chases to maintain their dominance over younger males. When the traps were set, the dominant males were among the first to be trapped. As soon as the door closed, a trapped animal would drop the bait that had just cost him his freedom and attempt to escape. Younger males outside the trap, some clearly subadult, would reach through the mesh of the trap and remove the dropped bait. No amount of threats, vocalizations, or other displays prevented a free animal from continued attempts until he met with success. As soon as the door of the trap drops, the dominance order changes. It might be interesting, however, to see what would happen if the trapped male were released!

Something about the troop's concern for infant baboons can be observed in trapping situations. One day, not long after my arrival in Kenya, I walked alone to one of my trapping areas. The traps were placed at the edge of a dense thicket. Most of the traps were empty and still set, but one trap held a female baboon and her infant. As I approached the traps, I could see members of the troop pacing back and forth within the underbrush. This was a common occurrence. Under most conditions the free animals react only with an occasional threat bark when the trapper carries sedated baboons from the traps. On this occasion, however, many threat barks were given when I attempted to sedate the mother. Each time the infant squealed, barks followed from the troop, and several large males ran toward the traps. Each time, the males came closer until they were only a few feet from me. Since this had never happened to me before, I really didn't know what to do. I could run, but I did not want to display my fear to the animals. I decided, if they really became determined, to go into an empty trap and close the door. It would be embarrassing, but safe. Before resorting to that extreme measure, I began to throw rocks at the threatening males and charged them back. Fortunately, the "naked ape" won the day.

On another occasion, I released an infant from a trap. The young animal ran in circles in a confused and terrified state. After a few moments, an adult male baboon ran into the clearing from the surrounding underbrush. Coming quite close to the humans nearby, he grabbed the black infant, allowed it to grasp his ventral hair, and then dashed back carrying it to the safety of the thicket. The incident very clearly illustrated the importance of the infant to the troop and how adult males protect the young. Even an activity such as trapping can be an enlightening experience.

Background in cultural anthropology, although useful to furnish comparative information on primate behavior, proved even more important in day-to-day relations with the local African populations. These relations were usually of two types, involving employees of the primate facility as well as Africans living in the same area as nonhuman primate populations. A background in cultural anthropology helped me to understand viewpoints of the Africans and to avoid many problems in East Africa caused by the ethnocentric behavior of various European populations. Time after time, I found that a willingness to listen to the point of view of local people not only made relations more harmonious, but often made the operation of the primate center more efficient. I have always found the people of East Africa very friendly and cooperative as long as their rights were respected. No indigenous people objected to my interest in nonhuman primates. They were particularly eager for me to trap baboons, although certain tribes then wanted the trapped baboons as a meat source. Most of the Africans were openly amused that anyone would want to waste so much time watching or trapping monkeys.

During the first year, I learned the basic techniques of baboon trapping and even began to experiment with new methods and traps. I learned something about the ecology of the area where I worked (near Darajani) and became familiar with what could and could not be done safely in the African bush country. I learned the distribution of baboons in that immediate area. In summary, that first year provided me with the experience that most field investigators acquire during their first field trip. I became somewhat more experienced than most in handling nonhuman primates, since constant trapping operations provided many opportunities. In fact, I had so many opportunities that I spent a week in a hospital after a bite from an adult male baboon severed my ulnar artery.

Having concentrated my efforts in a limited geographical area, I lacked the versatility necessary to study various primate species in various places. The next two years in Africa, when we began to conduct trapping and sampling safaris over much of Kenya and Tanzania, gave me much additional experience. This background gave me the training that primate investigators need to make them truly independent and free from the captivity of game parks.

It is my contention that we must study nonhuman primates in as many different ecological contexts as possible before we can understand their behavior. In the case of man, cultural anthropologists have been doing this for quite some time, but primatologists tend to generalize about nonhuman primate behavior on the basis of relatively few field investigations, in some cases only a single, short-term investigation of a given species.

Game-park investigations obviously present more limited study situations than those not fettered by the boundaries of parks. What game park has baboons along the beach? What game park has baboons at an 8,600-foot altitude? What game park has the interaction of farmers and crop-raiding baboons? What game park has the interaction of colobus monkeys, sykes' monkeys, and baboons? To study situations such as these, it is necessary to leave game parks, and in some cases, go into isolated areas, far from hotels or towns. An experienced person in a primate facility should have the background to know where each proposed investigation could be conducted and have the skills to provide the logistics necessary to allow the investigation to proceed.

The manager of a primate facility in Africa receives many strange requests. Some are clearly beyond the scope of such a facility, such as requests for crocodile bile, elephant tarsal bones, ostrich eyes, ticks from elephants, and blood from various game birds. Other requests, although properly directed to a primate facility, should be discouraged, such as an order for one male and six female bushbabies to establish a breeding colony. Since these animals tend toward long-term pairing, a colony with that composition would result in much fighting but little reproduction.

On the other hand, primate facility personnel can often greatly facilitate planning and conducting research projects. They know where to obtain supplies, where to locate animals living under the desired study conditions, and where the researchers can stay; they can assist research parties in camping and locating water sources and advise them about research permits and several other pertinent licenses and formalities. These are just a few of the services that the primate center can offer to investigators without becoming actively involved in the research projects themselves.

The longer one works for primate centers, the more one acquires training "extras" such as competent photographic ability, the ability to pilot small aircraft and land in the many small bush strips inaccessible from the ground, useful contacts and informants, the administrative skills needed to keep a safari operation running smoothly, and the ability to care for and maintain field equipment and vehicles under East African field conditions. For example, I once replaced both broken front springs of a Land Rover with two small saplings wired into place. With long-term work in the field, the indigenous populations learn who you are and what you are doing. Not only does this prevent endless explanations of why you are there, but the Africans, usually intrigued with any project working with wild animals, volunteer information and assistance. It often seemed that my local name of *Baba Nyani*, which means "Father Baboon," had preceded me into new areas and guaranteed better local cooperation and tolerance.

Someday I would like to see a primate study center created in East Africa with the sole purpose of carrying out behavioral and biological sampling projects, its own as well as those of visiting scientists. Such a center could be established with minimal cost by some granting agency and equipped with surplus vehicles, traps, and other equipment from their own research projects as well as those funded by other agencies. It would, therefore, become a pool for much of the equipment that is needlessly duplicated on project after project. It would also provide a permanent (or long-term) staff, including one or two primatologists. Its staff could gather much more information about the East African nonhuman primates than the many short-term projects could, at the same time vastly assisting short-term projects to be more productive.

Natives and Anthropologists In Arkansas

Dan F. Morse

Since 1967 I have been charged with sampling and interpreting prehistoric behavior for the Arkansas Archeological Survey in northeast Arkansas.[1] Stationed at Arkansas State University in Jonesboro, I am the only professional anthropologist on the faculty. The local residents, native to Arkansas for the most part, consider the anthropologist an outsider and treat him with the same basic kind of scepticism reserved for outsiders by all societies. The central theme of this paper involves the relationship of people in northeast Arkansas—both natives and anthropologists—to prehistoric cultural remains. I will first discuss our justifications of the Arkansas Archeological Survey to the public. Then I will characterize some of the natives whom we have difficulty reaching in regard to our anthropological goals. Finally, I want to describe our own research designs in northeast Arkansas.

The Arkansas Archeological Survey archeologist is in daily contact with a variety of taxpayers and tax-paying philosophies. He must be prepared to demonstrate a need for his services to justify the Survey to the public. Following are general value categories within which the public can relate to the archeologist and his work.

Study of Man. Indians are tired, and rightly so, of being considered only as study objects or noble savages. It is true that their cultures, both historically and prehistorically, have contributed tremendously to the development of anthropology. It is also true, however, that they have been studied mainly to develop a science of man and not solely as Indians. In ethnographic parallelism in archeology, racial identity is not stressed or deemed significant. Technological, historical, and environmental data are used in setting up hypothetical models.

Our scientific colleagues on the university faculty can relate better to a scientific study of man than to a strict history of the Indians of northeast Arkansas. This is particularly true of the colleagues and students we deal with most, those in the physical and biological sciences. But what of the nonuniversity public?

Serious amateurs can relate to a scientific study of man, although many are deeply involved in history as well. One local amateur has helped the Survey considerably. In one case he surface-collected a series of sites to help pinpoint in time a projectile point type which we were naming (Morse 1970). This is one of the few amateurs I know who reads Margaret Mead and tries to apply her writings to contemporary life.

The Arkansas Archeological Society (not to be confused with the Survey) is open to anyone who pays his dues. It includes serious amateurs and collectors as well. Its 1971 membership was 795, of which 494 were Arkansas residents. The best description of what the amateur can do is outlined in "The Role of the Amateur in Arkansas Archeology" by Charles A. Figley (1969:9–11). Following are some of the highlights of that paper:

> Let us first view the amateur in his role as a part of the general population, as opposed to the academic or the scientific community. In such a position, and because of the numerical strength of the amateurs, they can exert a tremendous impact regarding the status of archeology upon the mass mind of the State.
>
> Perhaps the greatest impact is made through private conversations. ... Articles appeared in State newspapers.... Exhibits ... were displayed at fairs and other public gatherings.... Books and publications ... were donated to public and school libraries.... Collections were catalogued and loaned for display in city and county museums ... civic, social, and service clubs had programs presented on archeology by amateurs....
>
> [There are] monthly meetings ... annual meetings ... [e]xcavations emphasizing proper scientific procedures ... [and] ... a lending library comprised of books not readily available elsewhere....
>
> One of the most time-consuming and vital areas of information required in Arkansas archeology is the location and reporting of sites within the State.... In addition to the information contained in the site report forms, several thousand artifacts from these sites have been donated.

... Individuals and groups of amateurs have offered valuable and time-saving assistance on professionally conducted surveys, ... [and] contributed ... volunteer labor ... by washing and cataloguing artifacts. ... Arkansas Society members have helped in professional digs. ... Information from private digs or surface finds has been made available to the professional through publications and oral reports. ... In short, the amateur has functioned as an extension of the eyes, ears, and legs of the professional. He has made available time, funds, and muscle, and has demonstrated to the professional that someone else does care.

Conservation. Probably our most important justification to the public lies in the need for preserving historical resources and ecologies on paper and film and for artifact recovery in the face of urban expansion and technological advances in farming. In fact, these needs essentially enabled the Arkansas Archeological Survey to come into being (Davis 1967). However, the meaning of the word *conservation* is different for different individuals (for example, contrast the meaning used by the Soil Conservation Service and by an ecologist). One unfortunate result of this difference is that leads to sites are not passed on to the archeologist when individuals feel that projects might be discouraged or slowed down because of archeological "interference." On the other hand, we have had a very satisfactory relationship with a land-leveler who also was concerned with conservation. In situations like this, the archeologist must be able to demonstrate that he will not significantly interfere with a project. District 10 of the Arkansas Highway Department has gone out of its way to cooperate with the Survey, probably because we early demonstrated that we could hold interference to a minimum. In addition, our association with Arkansas State University helped, since notes and artifacts were to be kept in the region where they were collected and not transported across the state to Fayetteville.

Many of our native informants for site locations and archeological finds are concerned more with conservation than with the study of man. Most dislike seeing areas cleared of woods and altered for farming and construction. They have a sense of history and sincerely wish to help the state of Arkansas preserve some of its past. These people often hold the next value as well.

Primitive Technology. People who hunt, fish, or observe wildlife as a hobby can best relate to us with this value. Natives who live close to the land can experience a spiritual kinship with prehistoric peoples and with anthropologists. One landowner was at best permissive of our efforts to excavate on his land until I began to ask him how deer might be hunted and butchered with stone age implements. He explained to me later that he would never understand why some of his acquaintances picked up points and glued them in frames to hang on walls. But he could understand what we were doing and furthermore felt it was worthwhile. Several times when a landowner or tenant has asked why we picked up a bunch of rocks, I have emptied a specimen bag and gone over every fragment to demonstrate the kind of inferences we could make from them. One landowner then calmly asked me if some of the rocks had been heated to make them easier to work. I have learned that you cannot underestimate native intelligence.

Hard Work. Most farmers—and we work in a basically rural environment—have a strong value for working hard. Such a farmer can relate to the archeologist who works hard and long hours. He also feels that since we work hard, the task must be worthwhile. During one salvage job, we were pleasantly embarrassed by the owner's son-in-law, who kept bringing people by and exclaiming that we were the hardest working state employees he had ever seen, and that we did not stop until it got dark. In a way, our job is similar to the farmer's, since we are our own boss, and we do want to get the job done quickly and efficiently.

Local Revenue and Publicity. Scientific meetings at and noncontroversial publicity for Arkansas State University allow the school administration and the Jonesboro Chamber of Commerce to relate more easily to the archeologist. The Mid-South Archeological Conference, held in Jonesboro in 1971, slightly increased local revenue and gave the school some good scholarly publicity. Every month the local chapter of the Arkansas Archeological Society meets on campus, with newspaper publicity. Almost every dig is covered by local newspapers—one dig, even by television—and the *Jonesboro Sun* occasionally features excellent stories on the Survey's activities. I talk to service clubs, science classes, junior high civic classes, university history, geology, and agriculture classes, the Presbyterian Church Friendship Group, county historical associations, the Junior Chamber of Commerce, and a variety of similar groups.

Recently the American Indian movement has begun to make our work controversial. However, since we work in an area where most natives can claim Indian ancestry, we do not expect the value of publicity to backfire.

In 1971 the foreman of a large farm (they are not called "plantations" anymore) asked me some questions about some aboriginal remains we were salvaging from a knoll which was being graded as a part of northeast Arkansas' farming improvement program. Did they speak a language? Did they really get married and live in families? Were they people? Soon afterward, I was looking at some nineteenth-century clay pipes in a curio cabinet filled with a variety of "Indian relics." The owner and his wife quickly assured me that those were "people pipes," and not Indian.

There is a large body of natives we as anthropologists never or almost never reach in explaining our goals and interests. These people cluster into three major categories: collectors, apathists, and creedsmen. People in all three categories believe that anthropologists are outsiders.

Collectors. People collect for a number of reasons. This section does not include the serious amateur. Grave robbers are very numerous in northeast Arkansas. They usually fall into two groups, although little difference can be detected in the field. The people in one group are, in essence, "pack rats." Huge amounts of unrecorded material, mostly pots and projectile points, are stacked on curio shelves, glued on walls, and stashed in boxes around various parts of the house. Oddly enough, a large number of these people are schoolteachers who in some cases literally trade grades for artifacts or take pupils out to help rob graves. In some schools, social studies is actually taught as grave-robbing. These collectors often proudly tell you they do not sell. But spouses have told me *they* have sold artifacts, and a great deal of trading goes on. Some of these collectors do little or no digging, being content to surface-collect.

Collectors are on the increase (Coggins 1972; Davis 1972). The psychological urge to own things other people covet is strong and contagious. In addition, leisure time and money has created a desire to look middle class by possessing items denoting conspicuous consumption. There may also be an unconscious attempt to get back at the government by destroying information. Furthermore, these items are regarded as good investments, and there is little doubt that prices—at least between collectors—have gone up at an alarming rate. Unesthetic Mississippi Valley pots sell from $5 to $1,000 apiece. Prices ranging from $40 to $500 have been paid while the pot was still dirty. Pot-hunting groups are organized in some instances to dig a site out as completely as possible. A fairly highly placed state official is involved in one of these groups, and numerous lesser state employees participate in organized and unorganized grave-robbing. The high prices have created a category of vandals who dig for "fun and profit." This is not a new phenomenon but has increased due to the increase of collectors with leisure money. Possibly as many as two hundred and fifty people are involved in grave-robbing in northeast Arkansas and another thousand or more surface-collect for profit. We suspect that many of the people involved do not report the transactions on their income tax returns. Last month over sixty-five diggers showed up at one site when word got out that same day that digging was allowed. An estimated eight hundred pots were found in three and a half weeks. I have watched human bone broken up and scattered over the surface so that the sounding rods would not strike that grave again. One digger even covered his sounding rod with luminous paint to be able to dig at night.

To handle the volume, a series of dealers or middlemen have sprung up. One "town" has a single gas station and two dealers. One dealer has two field men who go from house to house looking for things to buy. There are probably about a dozen or more dealers in the northeast corner of Arkansas. Larger dealers operate from the fringe—in Tennessee, Missouri, Illinois, Ohio, and Kentucky—among them being a fairly highly placed federal official. The archeologist gets dizzy just trying to follow up an important find. Most dealers are reluctant to do more than simply show you their wares lest you cut off the supply. They will show you some of the items hoping to identify a rare artifact unrecognized by them.

Who buys these specimens from the secondary dealers? For each time an artifact is sold, its price must be doubled to bring in an "adequate profit." Some better homes display the artifacts as decorations, although the trend is still toward Meso American and Southwestern material (Forester 1971). Dilettanti with excessive leisure money buy large quantities of the higher priced items. They seem like a transplant from the Renaissance filling their curio cabinets with strange and wondrous things. A large number of medical doctors are in this group as well as lawyers and business executives. Among these collectors, the sole criterion for an object's worth is how much it can be sold for. Provenience is not very important. There is almost no conception of historical or scientific value. No one seems to realize that virtually each object symbolizes a robbed grave or some similar act of vandalism against mankind. We rarely mention that thought when we interact with such collectors for fear of cutting off a source of information. Besides, in over fifteen years, I have never converted a true collector.

Apathists. Every dig attracts hordes of visitors. We average two hundred a week when the site is accessible and has received some publicity. Invariably, there is a morbid curiosity to "see a dead Indian." We now keep skeletons covered with plastic sheets until we can remove them with minimal damage for laboratory processing and storage. Since most of our skeletons have been uncovered by farm or construction machinery, we do not usually have sufficient material for a good physical anthropological study. We simply "rescue" the skeleton from being scattered around the field and bits from ending up in local curio boxes.

Howard Pierce, head of the Mathematics Department at Jonesboro High School and originator of the state's first formal high school archeology club, asked approximately ninety students in his classes what they thought about archeology. Five responded that they did not really think much about it. But eighty-five did not even care enough to say they did not care!

Much of the population seems apathetic to our goals. Some may be curious at a given moment but most simply do not care. Landowners destroy sites without telling us after being asked to contact us before leveling them. Some thought we were really not interested or that the site was not an important one. A proprietor of a store near an excavation refused a tour of the site for no other reason than complete apathy. Large groups of students walk past the open door of our archeological laboratory every year without even a glance inward. A landowner who prides himself on doing "good deeds" refused an archeological survey on his holdings until convinced we were not going to publish on his destructiveness of the environment. There is some self-interest involved but also, largely, plain apathy. But then, all people are apathetic toward something. Scientists do not always escape the label of apathists. In 1972, we have begun to record and investigate nineteenth-century sites including log cabins, early towns, cemeteries, and stoneware kilns. It will be interesting to see whether the apathy continues as we help unravel a history more personally pertinent to modern inhabitants of northeast Arkansas.

Creedsmen. In northeast Arkansas, we get a kind of generation gap between natives' and archeologists' beliefs about the past. This happens when a great deal of new scientific information is obtained in a short time, when there is a native dependence on oral tradition, and if there is very strong scepticism against outsiders not involved in local historic traditions. Oddly enough, there is also respect for science; hence we get a strange pattern of holding the creed while nodding politely as the scientist speaks.

Probably the best example concerns beliefs surrounding the New Madrid Earthquake of 1811–1812 (Fuller 1912; Saucier 1970). Despite clear evidence that the "sunk lands" were not sunk and that the lakes resulted from water being dammed downstream and filling extinct braided stream channels long before the earthquake took place, many local residents still talk and write about the "sunk lands" being caused by the earthquake. There is even an organization dedicated to this proposition. I have had a friend get very upset when I told her Indians were living along a lake almost nine hundred years before she thought it had been created.

There is not a great deal of difference between this sort of holding onto a creed and the history of the acceptance of fossil man by paleontologists and anthropologists during the past century. In 1856 the type fossil for Neanderthal was discovered. In the 1850s and 1860s a great deal of controversy surrounded its validity as a fossil, but by about 1890 Neanderthal was generally accepted as kin, if not actually ancestral, to modern man. In 1890 Dubois began to discover the Pithecanthropus fossils. By the end of the 1920s, acceptance was finally completed by the finds at Choukoutien. In 1924 Dart identified the Taung fossil, but general acceptance did not begin until the end of the 1940s and probably was not universally accepted until 1959–1960 with Leakey's finds at Olduvai Gorge. There is a pattern of thirty-five to forty years between the introduction of a new creed or idea and its general acceptance. I detect a distinct parallel here between natives and anthropologists.

In Jonesboro the text used for fifth-grade social studies is *Our Arkansas* (Brown 1963). The twelve-page chapter "The Indians of Arkansas" includes a variety of erroneous statements probably based on sources which date from the late 1930s and 1940s. On the basis of the above pattern, can we expect an updated version within five to ten years?

When we first approached northeast Arkansas, our research design was not very refined. So little had been done, particularly on pre-Mississippi phases, that we could hardly help but learn from the start. However, we had to accommodate a bewildering array of data and had to select what we deemed pertinent for now. We stored what we did not use for later.

As the only archeologist in northeast Arkansas, I was responsible for reconstructing a chronological sequence of cultural stages and phases. There were no trained students and only minimal funds to obtain untrained help. I was responsible for all site mapping, all salvage, and all interagency contact for about 11,544 square miles. In addition I had begun to locate a variety of amateur and collector informants, each expecting my individual attention. Few archeologists appreciate the fantastic richness of this area in sites and artifacts. Many archeologists do understand the pressure of working an area which may have most or all of its archeological potential destroyed in ten to fifteen years (Medford 1972). Put together the richness and the ongoing destruction, and you can readily imagine the huge collections of artifacts that can be accumulated in a very short time. Add the lack of trained help and you can appreciate the absence of updated analyses. Much of our data is relatively unexplored. The nature of the sampling being what it had to be, much of the data may even be extremely limited as to potential use.

Following Jelinek's paper concerning methodology (n.d.), I attempted to control the variables of culture, ecology, and chronology. Luckily we had the advantage of established sequences in neighboring states, and a cultural sequence could be quickly outlined since it involved more a verification of an expected model than a beginning from scratch. Our main concern was to identify the major developmental stages, see the nature of variability of each stage, and to modify our thoughts on the expected technological aspects. We literally "grabbed" samples any way and anywhere we could. Surface collections were made of all tools, a variety of stone debitage, and all visible decorated and rim sherds. Whenever possible other collections from the concerned sites were seen. Most of these sites were being walked by a large number of collectors at the same time that we were trying to get our samples. Some sites were selected by us to be collected from at various times of the year. Many site samples consist of what could be collected behind a dirt buggy or bulldozer. We have no illusions concerning the rather severe interpretative limitations of these samples. Control by excavation on a large scale is the obvious next step.

The chronological ordering of these collections and sites was relatively easy, since again we could use the results of neighboring sequences and seriation. Assuming that similar assemblages and similar artifact patterns are closer together in time, we cross-dated from the established sequences. In some cases stratigraphic verification was possible. In 1967 and 1968 we were involved in a significant contradiction. We were collecting artifacts which logically dated to three main periods between eight thousand and thirteen thousand years ago. The accepted earliest age of the land surfaces from which these tools were being collected, some in large numbers, was only four thousand to six thousand years. We were very reluctant to accept these late dates since it would throw doubt on the logic involved in the chronological ordering of our whole sequence. Fortunately, Roger Saucier (1968) published a new Mississippi Valley developmental hypothesis which revised dates, leaving us more than enough time for our early man material. Some verification of later events was involved as well. Radiocarbon dates have helped in ordering major parts of the later sequences. But such dates ordinarily are of little use in ordering developmental steps within an archeological phase. We have collected archaeomagnetic samples, and helped begin an investigation to establish a dendrochronology based on the bald cypress for the Lower Mississippi Valley. These techniques will help a great deal if successful.

The ecological variable is the most difficult to control. There were claims of geological changes associated with the New Madrid Earthquake of 1811–1812. We hoped to find undisturbed sites buried by the earthquake. The possibility of earthquake disturbance, however, severely limited specific ecological reconstruction. We first attempted to locate large, undisturbed sites in the "sunk lands," with negative results. In fact, larger sites post-dating A.D. 900 are located along the edges of these lakes. This caused us to begin questioning the origin of the "sunk lands" and a number of other topographical patterns assigned to the earthquake. Saucier (1970) once again came to our rescue, and we were able to disregard earthquake activity as a significant modifier of the local topography. Saucier's (1964) and Smith and Saucier's (1971) geological maps of this region allowed us even better geological control. Plotting mastodon finds indicated woodland or parkland environment, and we felt the relict braided stream channels would have been ponded at the end of the Pleistocene. Extrapolation backward in time from the present indicated hardwoods, and a high deer population could be inferred. We have not been able to do much more than the above on ecological reconstruction.

By the end of 1969 we had fulfilled the basic goals set in late 1967 (Morse 1969a) and moved into a new orientation. A hypothesis concerning the settlement pattern and economic behavior of Dalton culture (8,000–10,000 years ago) in northeast Arkansas was developed, and predictions of artifacts to be found were made to test the hypothesis (Morse 1971). A total of 250 sites were reviewed and 3PO139 selected as the potentially best site for the test. Al Goodyear of the University of Arkansas was invited to participate in return for an M.A. thesis topic (Goodyear 1971). This allowed us to fund the excavation and we were able to hire five graduate and undergraduate students from four institutions. As it was, only a small part of the site could be excavated since a large number of artifacts and stone debitage were found in a natural level. Essentially the hypothesis was verified as well as modified. A great deal more work needs to be done with new hypotheses developed as a result of that excavation (Morse 1972). The rest of the site must be excavated and another selected for extensive tests to verify the pattern. A different site must be tested with different artifacts predicted. Extensive, controlled surface collections must be made and a sample area of the drainage extensively surveyed. The pattern must be verified in another drainage area and possible differences between apparent family bands investigated. The only trouble is funding the project, for this is the only way to get trained personnel. A similar problem-oriented project now has been initiated for the other end of the time scale, the Nodena phase of A.D. 1400–1700.

There are a variety of reasons for conducting salvage work on an archeological site. In each case, however, the archeologist must ask himself: why, how, how long, and when. Two examples are appropriate here.

Site 3LW106 was a middle Mississippi (Wilson phase) farmstead. A friend of the son-in-law of the owner, who was grading the site, contacted me because he, the son-in-law, and I are on the Arkansas State University faculty. It was obvious that bad public relations would occur if I told him the truth—that I was actually too busy to salvage a site just then. The site was already partly destroyed, so the salvage had to be done that week. By directing the dirt buggy, we could scrape large areas for possible features and quickly get an overall view. We also could concentrate on a twice-rebuilt house. A week was the absolute maximum we could spend at the site. Such a salvage project has side benefits. The student assistants can make field mistakes with minimal consequences, have a second and third chance within hours, and see a whole site unravel within days. During the excavation, visitors often provide excellent leads to other sites, collections, and informants. Sometimes it is beneficial to continue an instant salvage job even though there is relatively little return in information or artifacts. The archeologist is involved in a constantly shifting pattern of priorities and on-the-spot decisions. If we do not respond to a request from a land modifier, we are saying in effect that the state or university simply does not care. Because of the personalities of the owners, we have even continued salvage jobs beyond our immediate academic needs. Sometimes we have discontinued or not begun salvage projects with a great deal of potentially new information. I am satisfied that we are salvaging at our maximum capacity.

Another type of salvage job appears when the site is of major importance and there is more time to salvage. A preliminary survey revealed three sites which were in danger of being destroyed by the Corps of Engineers. Permission to test all three was obtained, and in 1968 two assistants and I spent a month, with state funds, doing the testing (Morse 1968). One site (3MS20) was discovered to be unique and relatively undisturbed. The other two sites were related but already were mostly destroyed by construction activities. At 3MS20, not only were unique artifacts recovered, but a section of the site was discovered to be stratified. On the basis of these tests, a National Park Service grant was obtained for more extensive salvage. We had a year to decide how to excavate and how to extract the most information (Morse 1969b). A great deal was learned about initial Mississippi culture in northeast Arkansas, and a large quantity of artifacts and notes resulted that I still have not been able to digest. We are now trying to save the site but, if unsuccessful, will have to do more salvage work there because additional finds, important to test ideas derived from the previous excavations, await us.

The modern residents of northeast Arkansas share with the prehistoric inhabitants a common cultural ancestry. Two million years or more of cultural evolution took place before Indians migrated into the Americas with a tool kit basically not dissimilar from that in use in Europe in the Upper Paleolithic. In addition, there is clear evidence of a sophisticated, orderly life in prehistoric Arkansas. Yet, many modern residents will not acknowledge their human kinship with Indians; worse, some really do not care. To change these apathetic attitudes, we will have to convince people that social studies in the primary and secondary school system must be legitimatized. Social studies in northeast Arkansas schools, I have discovered, is history and nothing more unless an exceptional teacher enlarges it. Controversy is minimized in most school systems. Anthropology, sociology, geography, and political science are names only seen in the newspaper or a college bulletin. Given this background, how can we expect natives to relate to broken stones lying around on the ground other than apathetically or as potential treasure?

Our archeological research must become more systematized. "Grab samples" can only be used so far, and, considering the present conditions of sites, I doubt that much better samples can be obtained without excavating on a large scale. Grave-robbing and a variety of sophisticated farming techniques have probably thwarted any attempt on our part to collect a controlled surface sample. But we must test this "feeling" by excavation.

We have developed a number of specific research proposals to be investigated and will develop yet more in the near future. Our stored collections must be categorized and the information stored in the computer at Fayetteville for wider dissemination. The public must be reached not only to give them a greater understanding of human behavior and an appreciation of other peoples in other times, but to help protect the data we need so badly. Our results may not "guide the future." But if we wish greater understanding of cultural processes we must act now to investigate some of the most important prehistoric remains now available before they are lost forever.

NOTE

1. For a history and description of the Arkansas Archeological Survey, see Davis 1967, 1969.

REFERENCES

Brown, Walter L., 1963. *Our Arkansas*. (Austin: Steck-Vaughn).

Coggins, Clemency, 1972. Archeology and the Art Market. *Science* 175:263–266.

Davis, Hester A., 1967. *The Arkansas Archeological Survey*, Field Notes, No. 28 (Fayetteville). (Monthly Newsletter of the Arkansas Archeological Society.)

————, 1969. A Brief History of Archeological Work in Arkansas up to 1967. *Arkansas Archeologist* 10:2–8.

————, 1972. The Crisis in American Archeology. *Science* 175:267–272.

Figley, Charles A., 1969. The Role of the Amateur in Arkansas Archeology. *Arkansas Archeologist* 10:9–11.

Forester, Leslie R., 1971. Decorate with Art. *Family Circle* 79(5):85–87.

Fuller, Myron L., ed., 1912. *The New Madrid Earthquake*. United States Geological Survey, Bulletin 494 (Washington, D.C.).

Goodyear, Albert C., 1971. The Brand Site: The Dalton Tool Kit with an Intrasite Analysis. (M.A. thesis, University of Arkansas, Fayetteville.)

Jelinek, Arthur J., n.d. Prehistory: World, Methodology. (Manuscript on file at the Museum of Anthropology, University of Michigan).

Medford, Larry D., 1972. Agricultural Destruction of Archeological Sites in Northeast Arkansas. *Arkansas Archeological Survey, Research Series* No. 3:41–82.

Morse, Dan F., 1968. Preliminary Report on 1968 Archeological Excavations at the Big Lake National Wildlife Refuge. (Report prepared for the Department of the Interior, Washington, D.C., by the Arkansas Archeological Survey.)

————, 1969a. Introducing Northeastern Arkansas Prehistory. *Arkansas Archeologist* 10:12–28.

————, 1969b. Preliminary Report on Archeological Excavations at the Zebree Site (3MS20) Summer 1969. (Report prepared for the Department of the Interior, Washington, D.C., by the Arkansas Archeological Survey.)

————, 1970. The Big Creek Point. *Central States Archaeological Journal* 17:20–23.

————, 1971. Recent Indications of Dalton Settlement Pattern in Northeast Arkansas. *Proceedings of the Twenty-Seventh Southeastern Archaeological Conference* 13:5–10.

————, 1972. Dalton Culture in Northeast Arkansas. *Florida Anthropologist*, in press.

Saucier, Roger T., 1964. *Geological Investigation of the St. Francis Basin*. U.S. Army Engineer Waterways Experiment Station, Technical Report No. 3–659 (Vicksburg).

————, 1968. A New Chronology for Braided Stream Surface Formation in the Lower Mississippi Valley. *Southeastern Geology* 9:65–76.

————, 1970. Origin of the St. Francis Sunk Lands, Arkansas and Missouri. *Geological Society of America Bulletin* 81:2847–2854.

Smith, F. L., and R. T. Saucier, 1971. *Geological Investigation of the Western Lowlands Area Lower Mississippi Valley*. U.S. Army Engineer Waterways Experiment Station, Technical Report S–71–5 (Vicksburg).

Museums as Anthropological Data Banks

WILLIAM C. STURTEVANT

FOR ABOUT 450 years Europeans and Euroamericans have been gathering exotic artifacts along with specimens of natural history.[1] As the Age of Exploration and of colonial expansion progressed, European Cabinets of Curiosities grew larger, attracted much popular interest, and in the latter half of the eighteenth century gradually became public museums. Independent museums of anthropology and formal anthropology departments within natural history and historical museums date from about 1840 in Europe; in the United States the major anthropological museums for the most part began in the 1870s. Both often incorporated the remnants of earlier collections. By now there may be some four or five million ethnological specimens in the museums of the world, including somewhat over one and a half million in United States museums. Of these last probably half are in the ten or twelve largest museums while the rest are very widely scattered.[2]

Perhaps half or more of the ethnological specimens in American museums are of North American Indian origin. The present discussion will focus on these, although similar points could be made about ethnological collections from other parts of the world. Note, however, that concentration on ethnological collections results in an incomplete presentation, for the nature and status of archeological and physical anthropological collections are significantly different.

Although anthropological collections grew up with the natural history collections where many of them are still housed, museum specimens have never been central to anthropological research—whereas in botany, mammology, or paleontology, even now the care of museum collections is readily justified on the basis of present and past research. If current research in these fields does not usually center in museums, nevertheless the very names and identifications of the organisms studied usually rest ultimately on museum specimens. Although museums are among the very few institutions able to support anthropologists as full-time or nearly full-time research workers, it is sad but true that even the great majority of museum ethnologists who are actively engaged in research do not study the collections under their care.[3]

Although our collections are little studied, the North American Indian ones especially are now very popular. The objects in them are in much demand for temporary exhibitions in art galleries, and in other ways also they are being pulled into the strange art world where public museums, private collections, and the commerce that serves them are interlocked, with the curators, directors, and governing boards of museums intermingled, interchanging, and functionally interrelated with dealers and private collectors. Many of the most important anthropological museums are now participating in the art market. Unique objects that have never been adequately studied are leaking away and becoming separated from their documented histories as they pass from public museums into private collections, often via dealers and auction houses.[4] If more anthropologists were studying these collections, curators and museum directors would be less likely to let them go.

The reasons for the lack of study are complex and difficult to understand. But indubitably in social anthropology/ethnology the study of cultural materials (that is, artifacts) lags very seriously behind the study of cultural behavior and belief, cognition, or perception. Yet man is preeminently a tool-using animal, one that cannot survive without the artifacts which link him to his environment. Human ecology and economics begin with artifacts, and all else is merely superstructure. It should be a matter of some urgency for anthropology that the spread of Westernization, of industrialization and its mass-produced goods, is wiping out distinct local technologies and arts even more rapidly than it is decreasing the variety of languages, forms of social organization, and religions. We are rapidly losing irreplaceable opportunities for field research on technology and on esthetics, and for preserving documentation of the variety that yet survives by means of the sophisticated collecting for museums that should accompany field research.

One symptom of the lag in research on material culture is the age of the standard sources. In this area, any bibliography or reading list will have to include publications dating back several decades, and some of the standard reference sources date from around 1900 or even before. We still have nothing to replace Otis T. Mason's monograph on North American baskets (1904) or Gudmund Hatt's standard work on moccasins (1916), and there are dozens of other examples for North America alone.[5] Among the best field studies, which still should be cited as models, are Lila O'Neale's monograph on Yurok-Karok basket weavers (1932) and Ruth Bunzel's work on Pueblo pottery decoration (1929). Cornelius Osgood's exhaustive description of the material inventory of the Ingalik was published in 1940; no work done since then equals that in the systematic detailed description of each artifact and in the exhaustive coverage of all known types.[6] To cite an example from another part of the world, Petr Bogatyrev's monograph on the folk costume of Moravian Slovakia, published in Slovak in 1937, has just in 1971 appeared in English translation, despite the importance of its author in the Prague and Moscow linguistic circles and in the early development there of structural ethnography and formalist approaches to folklore and literature. The work still makes a methodological contribution and only seems somewhat old-fashioned in its mixing of structural with historical statements.

More and better ethnography focused on artifacts and on folk esthetics is needed quickly. Our vast museum collections can serve as adjuncts to such field studies, yet too often even those few field workers who do study material culture do not make adequate use of existing museum specimens as sources of data. In addition, much useful research can be conducted using museum collections with little or no fresh field study. Almost any ethnographic research can benefit from an examination of museum collections. It should be standard practice to study these holdings just as one does library and archival materials both before and after beginning ethnographic fieldwork. Knowledge derived from fieldwork is a great help in identifying and interpreting museum specimens; on the other hand, field inquiries based on knowledge of older artifacts in museums—and on photographs of them—often add data that would otherwise be lost (see Fenton 1967). Newton's study (1971) of Timbira cotton fabrics is a recent demonstration of the advantages of alternating in this way between field and museum research.

Suitable topics for museum research are limited by variables of space, time, and artifact type. Worldwide or continental coverage requires a focus on a well-defined type or technique. Here belong especially the basic studies that improve and rationalize descriptive techniques, to which one can refer as guides and standards for both field and museum descriptions. The fundamental etics for most artifact categories are badly in need of elucidation by reexamination of a very wide range of museum specimens coupled with a search of the previous descriptive and classificatory literature. When one is faced by a basket, or a woven fabric, or a bead, how should one begin to describe it? For these, as for few other categories, we do have good descriptive standards in modern works to which students should be directed. Basketry descriptions should begin with Balfet's standards (1952); the etics of woven fabrics have been thoroughly described and exemplified by Emery (1966); and any study of glass bead types ought to refer to the Kidds' work (1970). Other useful models for improving descriptive standards can be found in the archeological literature and in much work on classification altogether outside anthropology.

Most other types of museum research require well-documented specimens. One must at least begin with a core of objects of known provenience and known date. Once a series like this has been established, the corpus can sometimes be enlarged by adding other objects that are less clearly documented but that can now be identified typologically by comparison with the well-documented skeleton. Whether or not one can gather a corpus of sufficient size to yield significant results depends partly on the time period under study. Objects made before about 1800 from most parts of the world are the incunabula of ethnological collections: they are so rare that each one deserves careful separate description, but they tend to be of scientific value only when their typicality can be gauged by comparing them with the more extensive collections from later times, or if they can be related to archeological finds. More objects survive from the nineteenth century, but for many parts of the world, it is not until one reaches the period of massive and careful field collecting—perhaps 1880–1920—that sufficient collections exist to allow detailed study of a wide range of artifact types from one society or group of societies. Ethnological studies of artifacts of the period since about 1920 will usually depend heavily on field ethnography, since if examples have not been kept, the memory of their construction and uses survives, while many of the specimens that have been collected will still be in private hands rather than in museums.

A study of artifacts ought to be based on a wide search for relevant data. The collections of a single museum—even one of the largest—are rarely adequate for a specific study. An historian working with written documents will investigate the holdings of many repositories, and so should the historian and anthropologist dealing with objects. It is a common failing, especially in North Americanist studies, to limit the search to nearby institutions—for important materials are usually widely dispersed. Thus, for example, the best collections of Pueblo artifacts of the late nineteenth century are not in the Southwest but in Washington, New York, Chicago, and Cambridge, with some important examples as far afield as Leiden and Göteborg. Tools to locate collections are not adequate. A survey by Hunter (1967) is helpful but does not include all relevant museums and the answers that curators gave to Hunter's inquiries were usually not very specific. A project for a really detailed union catalog of ethnological holdings (Ricciardelli 1967) has so far covered only the museums of Oklahoma and Missouri (the punchcards and computer printouts are kept at the Stovall Museum in Norman). Kaemlein's (1967) very thorough inventory of Southwestern collections in Europe ought to be imitated for other kinds of materials. However, the researcher must usually depend on correspondence and on visits to locate materials relevant to his interests.[7]

The choice of a topic suitable for museum research should depend not only on the availability of objects but also on the kind of information accompanying the specimens, on the catalog data. The ideal quality of cataloguing, in the field and in the museum (cf. Sturtevant 1966, 1967a; Borhegyi 1965), is rarely met with. Only a small proportion of museum objects has been collected by professional anthropologists or trained collectors, and an even smaller proportion is accompanied by the detailed data one could gather in fieldwork focused on artifacts. There is no point in proposing a museum study of folk classifications, or of ethnoesthetics, or of attitudes about objects, or of the detailed relations between material culture and social organization, for the data do not exist in museums. Many objects arrived in museums without any accompanying information whatsoever and are now associated with data added (usually anonymously) on typological grounds. Such information must always be checked and often requires correction. Feest's Law of Museum Documentation holds: The uncertainty of an attribution increases with the square of the distance from the collector's statements (Feest 1968:145). It is reasonable to expect museum documentation to cover some of the following information about an artifact—in decreasing order of probability of occurrence: Where the item is from (the culture or region); its general type (a name is given to it, according to its function or technique of manufacture or material); the date it was received in the museum (much less frequently, the date collected; very rarely, the date made); its constituent materials, or some of them (very often provided by the museum cataloguer rather than the collector, and it is usually difficult to determine by which of them). These are the basic features of documentation on which the research must depend. It is rarer to find information on such topics as the name of the field collector (important for evaluating the data), the native name for the object, its cost or how it was obtained, the specific locale from which it comes, its particular function, its individual history, or its meaning or iconography.

The museum catalog is like a bad index in a book: it helps a lot but should not be trusted to be complete or accurate. Studying museum collections requires both examining and describing the artifact itself, and searching out and evaluating the information about it which is in the museum. Often the latter task takes at least as much time as the former. The museum staff must be interviewed about its specific systems of record-keeping. If there is a card catalog, how is it arranged and indexed? What lies behind it—old book catalogs, manuscript or typed? Are there duplicate catalogs (sometimes different information has been added to them)? Have there been changes in the numbering system? What sorts of accession papers exist? Among possibilities to be investigated are business papers, correspondence, shipping papers, bills, receipts, and especially field catalogs and original collectors' lists and catalogs. Such materials are often kept in more than one location: near the catalogs, or in the library, archives, department office, registrar's office, old safes and closets. Old museum photographs of the objects may contain information that now appears nowhere else. Often there is writing on the objects themselves or on attached tags or labels that is significant both directly and through the handwriting style or the type of old numbers. Finally, most museums have some exceptions to the usual plan of storage; one should ask whether any special collections or special types of artifacts are separated from the rest (e.g., very long or large or valuable objects, or the earliest collections).[8]

Contextual studies are best based mainly on field studies, and may be typified by the volumes in two excellent recent publication series: "Art in its Context" edited by Adrian Gerbrands, and "Art and Society" edited by Peter J. Ucko. Such studies treat the relation between the objects and some nonartifactual aspect such as social structure, ritual, psychology, or the character and life history of individual artists. Formal studies, on the other hand, treat the context as given and analyze the objects themselves. They may be conducted in the field (and there are usually advantages to field study) but they may often also be carried out on the basis of museum specimens, while some sorts of formal study require museum collections alone.

I would urge the usefulness and the interest of what is sometimes disparaged as "mere connoisseurship" and what Robert McC. Adams has called "a kind of philately of art styles or material objects" in contrast to the scientific emphases of the new archeology (Adams 1968). One can welcome the developments that let us see how archeology is anthropology (Binford 1962) and still continue to be interested in the objects themselves, as concrete forms, and in their typology, distribution, styles, and esthetic aspects. There is room in anthropology for an approach to artifacts that corresponds to that of scholars of Western art and technology who value artifacts and study them as cultural products, not just as documents to yield evidence about less concrete aspects of culture and history. It could even be argued that it is ethnocentric to restrict to the products of Western cultures the history and criticism of art and the history of technology. At the same time, a strongly anthropological approach to artifacts has special values applicable also to the study of Western artifacts. The breadth of anthropological interests is appropriate here, as are the development of more objective descriptive techniques, the growth of rather sophisticated approaches to classification and typology (perhaps especially in archeology and ethnoscience), the strong tendency toward contextual studies, and sometimes dating based on seriation techniques and on controlled stratigraphic excavation. One sees the results readily enough in the contributions of anthropologists to the "artifact research" of the new and burgeoning field of historical archeology,[9] and the time may well be ripe for anthropologists to look seriously at European painting, sculpture, and architecture.

One aim of museum research is historical ethnography, the description of the material culture (or some aspect of it) of a given society at a given period in the past. There is a very large amount of useful work of this sort to be done, and it is easy to select projects of manageable size. Beyond simple description and compilation of artifact types is stylistic analysis: what are the features that characterize a style and its substyles, what distinguishes it from neighboring styles? Bill Holm's analysis of northern Northwest Coast art is a modern classic in this genre (1965). Efforts are increasing to identify the products of individual artists or craftsmen, even though their names are not known. This has long been successful in European art history and in classical archeology, but it is only relatively recently that anthropologists working with museum collections have begun to attempt it—there are some applications to West African sculpture, and more recently efforts are being made by several specialists to identify the works of individual Northwest Coast artists of the late nineteenth century (e.g. Duff 1967). Navajo weaving, Zuni and Hopi pottery, and many other extensively collected types would yield to this approach. The detailed attribute analysis of the new archeology is already leading archeologists to undertake ethnographic field studies of the work of individual potters, and certainly archeologists will increasingly apply and test their methods on ethnographic collections (see Dawson and Deetz 1965, for one example), just as ethnologists should pay more attention to archeologists' descriptive methods. Another model for stylistics is structuralism. Roland Barthes uses structuralist methods that are adaptable to the study of objects even though his fascinating study of French women's fashion magazines was limited to what they wrote about artifacts and avoided analysis of the forms of the artifacts themselves (Barthes 1967b; cf. Barthes 1967a). Structural approaches even more directly derived from linguistics, both the older item-and-arrangement style and the newer generative methods, can be seen in the work of a small group of Americans, most of whom are not yet applying the methods to museum collections.[10] Some of this work is done by a few linguists working on "two-dimensional languages" or "iconics," studying the structure of Chinese characters (Rankin 1965), cattle brands (Watt 1966–1967, 1967), chemical graphs, flow charts, and electronic circuits. Also related are Nancy Munn's work on Australian graphic signs (1962, 1966), and James Faris' beautiful analysis of the remarkable Nuba body painting (1972); both are field ethnographers not studying artifact categories represented in museums. Margaret Hardin Friedrich's important structural analyses of Tarascan pottery design are based on fieldwork, but her ethnography is documented in part by collections, very carefully sampled, made for the Field Museum; and her methods are relevant to the study of older collections (Friedrich 1970).

Museum materials are very suitable for historical studies of changes over time in style or in artifact types. Quite long sequences exist for many regions, providing the base for establishing hundreds of art histories. Here, too, models are provided by classical archeology (Rowe 1959) and the history of art (Kubler 1962). Carole Kaufmann (1969), studying the history of Haida argillite carvings, has recently provided a fine example of what can be done by applying art-historical and anthropological methods—including the componential analysis of composition—to ethnological museum collections.

The history of collecting and of museums is part of Euroamerican cultural and intellectual history that ought to be examined as evidence on the changing interests in exotic peoples and ideas about them. The evidence for such studies consists partly of written catalog and accession data that have often been overlooked as historical and ethnohistorical sources apart from the objects themselves. There are several hundred catalogs of Cabinets of Curiosities earlier than 1840, many of them published and many more in manuscript. Lach (1970: chap. 1) has recently shown what riches await investigation in the surviving inventories and descriptions of Asian curiosities in sixteenth-century European collections. Long ago David I. Bushnell, Jr., pointed out that Sir Hans Sloane's manuscript catalog, predating 1753, contains descriptions of eastern North American Indian objects that provide useful ethnohistorical data even when the original objects no longer survive in the British Museum (Bushnell 1906; see also Braunholtz 1953). A brief preliminary search shows that scraps of new information on Eastern Indian material culture can still be found in the catalog of the collections of the Royal Society (Grew 1681), in the catalog of Ole Worm's museum (which formed the nucleus of the National Museum in Copenhagen) (Worm 1655), and in the catalog of the Tradescants' collection (which went to Oxford via Elias Ashmole) (Tradescant 1656); further search would obviously be worthwhile, for historical ethnography and for European intellectual history.

A vast amount of data awaits anthropological research in the huge, tangled puzzles of museum collections. Like any large unexplored store, once one begins examining it one is rewarded with many new discoveries—although few indoor archeologists can expect to be so fortunate as Cranstone and Gowers (1968). They added to the small corpus of surviving Tahitian sculpture an important example collected by Captain James Cook on May 7, 1774. In 1966, when the British Museum dismantled for cleaning and restoration the mourner's costume which had been mounted on a cut-down European easel aboard the *Resolution* at Tahiti, they found folded Tahitian tapa cloth and, hidden inside the headdress, a fine carved wooden figure.

Museums are organized to facilitate research; their collections, records, and staffs are kept for that purpose and their ideals support research. In practice, research may be frustrated by low staffing, lack of space, lost specimens, mislaid records, and the demands of exhibit programs. But that is because research visitors are so infrequent. Museum research is often cheaper than fieldwork, and one can do useful work in short stretches of a few days or a week or two at a time. Anthropologists should be working in museums as historians do in archives and libraries: visiting nearby ones for odd moments during the working week, and traveling to more distant ones for research during vacations. Both the science and the profession of anthropology would benefit by much wider recognition of the usefulness of museums as data banks.

NOTES

1. I thank Philip J. C. Dark and John C. Ewers for useful criticisms of an earlier version of this paper.

2. For these estimates see Ricciardelli 1967 and Sturtevant 1969:640. Most totals of museum holdings are exaggerated, partly because catalog numbering series usually include archeological as well as ethnological specimens and those who estimate ethnological totals sometimes forget how rapidly the total increases as fragments from excavations are numbered. The largest anthropological collections in the United States are, in approximately the order of decreasing magnitude, those in the National Museum of Natural History, Smithsonian Institution (Washington, D.C.); the American Museum of Natural History (New York); the Museum of the American Indian, Heye Foundation (New York); the Field Museum of Natural History (Chicago); the Peabody Museum, Harvard University (Cambridge); the University Museum, University of Pennsylvania (Philadelphia); the Milwaukee Public Museum; the Lowie Museum of Anthropology, University of California (Berkeley); the Peabody Museum of Natural History, Yale University (New Haven); the Peabody Museum of Salem; and the Bernice P. Bishop Museum (Honolulu). Of the same order of

magnitude are the National Museum of Man (Ottawa) and the Royal Ontario Museum (Toronto).

3. See Sturtevant 1969 for a description of the current state of museum anthropology and some statistics on the history of studies of technology.

4. Canaday (1972a, 1972b) has pointed out that the public has at least an ethical interest in seeing that objects remain in the institutions which are given tax benefits for keeping them. This may explain why museums are usually secretive about sales of their holdings. Canaday advocates restricting sales to "competitive bidding limited to other American museums following full public announcement of the works to be sold." There is much evidence that anthropological materials are increasingly treated as fine art on the market. For example, the top price at an auction of "The Green Collection of American Indian Art" on November 19, 1971 at the Parke-Bernet Galleries in New York was $6,100, for a superb Washo basket made in 1905 by Datsolalee. The audience applauded as the item was knocked down at that figure—whereupon Harmer Johnson, who was conducting the sale, remarked "I thought that was reserved for famous paintings!"

5. Hirschberg et al. (1966) provide a useful summary of typologies on many areas of material culture, with some fresh systematization and many carefully selected bibliographies.

6. There are a few, but surprisingly few, recent monographic treatments of entire material cultures. Three important volumes by Koch (1961, 1965, 1971) are based almost entirely on fieldwork, as is LeBar's (1964) Trukese description. Kluckhohn's long-awaited monograph on *Navaho Material Culture* (Kluckhohn, Hill, and Kluckhohn 1971) is based on fieldnotes and also on museum collections, but the latter are not adequately used considering the quantity and quality of available materials, and in other ways also this volume is not as systematic and exhaustive as we had expected.

7. There are many published listings of museums which can provide leads, although all are inadequate. For North America, in addition to Hunter (1967), McGrath (1970) is essential, listing nearly all museums of all types but giving very little detail on their holdings or staff. Woodbury (1971) contains a directory of anthropological museums which is useful for providing the names and interests of the staffs but gives very little information on holdings and omits museums that do not employ anthropologists. For the United Kingdom, Anonymous (1971) is readily available and nearly complete but does not give much detail, while Museums Association (1971) is better. Equivalent lists of their museums are published in many other countries. Anonymous (1967) gives names and addresses of anthropological "Museums and Research Institutions" worldwide, but is quite incomplete and provides very little data on holdings and staffs. I have not seen any attempt to enumerate the Great Ethnological Collections of the world. Christian F. Feest, Adrienne L. Kaeppler, and T. J. Brasser have helped me to list "world class" institutions, to add to the ones in North America mentioned in note 2. Any really thorough search ought to query most of the following, in addition to museums in or near the area of origin of the artifacts to be studied (and in the present or former colonial metropolitan power): Department of Ethnography, British Museum (the offices and exhibits have moved from Bloomsbury to 6, Burlington Gardens, London W.1; research in the reserve collections will be difficult for a couple of years until they too have been moved); Musée de l'Homme (Paris); Museum für Völkerkunde (Berlin); Nationalmuseet (Copenhagen); Museum für Völkerkunde (Hamburg); Rijksmuseum voor Volkenkunde (Leiden); Pitt Rivers Museum (Oxford); Etnografiska Museet (Göteborg); Statens Etnografiska Museum (Stockholm); Linden-Museum für Völkerkunde (Stuttgart); Museum für Völkerkunde (Basel); Museum für Völkerkunde (Vienna); Staatliches Museum

für Völkerkunde (Munich); University Museum of Archaeology and Ethnology (Cambridge); Muzei Etnografiyi i Antropologiyi Akademiyi Nauk S.S.S.R. (Leningrad); Städtisches Museum für Völkerkunde (Frankfurt am Main); Rautenstrauch-Joest-Museum für Völkerkunde (Cologne); Museo Nazionale Preistorico ed Etnografico Luigi Pigorini (Rome); Náprstkovo Muzeum Asijských, Afrikých a Amerických Kultur (Prague); Horniman Museum (London); Staatliches Museum für Völkerkunde (Dresden); Museum für Völkerkunde (Leipzig); Sammlungen des Institutes für Völkerkunde (Göttingen); Museo Nazionale di Antropologia e Etnologia (Florence); Bernisches Historisches Museum (Berne); Hunterian Museum (Glasgow). More limited in geographical coverage but of the same order of magnitude are the ethnological collections of the Koninklijk Instituut voor de Tropen (Amsterdam), the Musée Royal de l'Afrique Centrale (Tervuren, near Brussels), and the Museo de América (Madrid; includes Oceanic as well as American materials). One must hope that the National Museum of Ireland will remain unique in its desire to remove itself from this class and discourage foreign visitors by "returning" its very important early collections from foreign lands in hopes of improving its holdings of Irish materials.

8. These comments have implications also for the amount of information that the museum staff can reasonably be expected to provide in response to a letter of inquiry (including the letter that should always precede the arrival of a scholar intending to study the collections). Most large museums can quite readily estimate approximately the number of objects they have from a specific culture, or the number of a rather general type of artifact from a given society. However, adequate indexes by type or function, across cultures, are rare—the Pitt Rivers Museum is probably unique among large museums in having the entire collection thus classified (see Blackwood 1970)—and really complete and reliable indexes of the museum's attributions by culture are also unusual (I have had good experiences with this kind of index in the Pitt Rivers Museum, the Yale Peabody Museum, and the Denver Art Museum's Department of Indian Art).

9. See, for example, articles in the annual *Historical Archaeology* published since 1967 by the Society for Historical Archaeology. A well-known and still exciting example of an anthropological approach to historical artifacts is the research on colonial New England gravestones conducted by Deetz and Dethlefson (e.g. Deetz and Dethlefson 1965, 1967; Dethlefson and Deetz 1966; Deetz 1968). Gilborn (1968) provides a different example.

10. The present writer has, however, worked out a rather simple componential analysis of Seminole shirts from museum specimens as well as field research (Sturtevant 1967b, prefigured in Sturtevant 1955). Conklin and Sturtevant (1953) in fieldwork among the Seneca applied an early version of emic analysis to the classification of musical instruments, while Ortiz (1952–1955) independently used an essentially emic basic typology for his magnum opus on Afro-Cuban musical instruments. Hymes (1970) has provided a very useful critical survey of the adaptation of linguistic methods of analysis to the study of artifacts.

REFERENCES

Adams, Robert McC., 1968. Archeological Research Strategies: Past and Present. *Science* 160: 1187–1192.

Anonymous, 1967. Fourth International Directory of Anthropological Institutions. *Current Anthropology* 8:647–751. (On pp. 733–737 is an alphabetical list of the "Museums & Research Institutions" and on pp. 741–751 is an index of all listed institutions by country.)

Anonymous, 1971. *Museums and Galleries in Great Britain and Ireland, 1971–2* (London: Index Publishers). (A new edition is published each July.)

Balfet, Hélène, 1952. La Vannerie: Essai de classification. *L'Anthropologie* 56:259–280. (Translated by M. A. Baumhoff as *Basketry: A Proposed Classification*, Papers on California Archaeology 47, pp.1–21, in University of California Archaeological Survey Reports No. 37, Berkeley, 1957.)

Barthes, Roland, 1967a. *Elements of Semiology*, translated by Annette Lavers and Colin Smith (London: Jonathan Cape). (First published as *Eléments de sémiologie*, Paris, 1964.)

———, 1967b. *Système de la Mode* (Paris: Editions du Seuil).

Binford, Lewis R., 1962. Archaeology as Anthropology. *American Antiquity* 28:217–225.

Blackwood, Beatrice, 1970. *The Classification of Artifacts in the Pitt Rivers Museum, Oxford*, Pitt Rivers Museum, University of Oxford, Occasional Papers on Technology 11 (Oxford).

Bogatyrev, Petr, 1971. *The Functions of Folk Costume in Moravian Slovakia*, Translated by Richard G. Crum. Approaches to Semiotics 5 (The Hague: Mouton). (First published in 1937 as *Funkcie kroja na Moravskom Slovensku.*)

Borhegyi, Stephan de, 1965. Curatorial Neglect of Collections. *Museum News* 43(5):34–40.

Braunholtz, H. J., 1953. The Sloane Collection: Ethnography. *British Museum Quarterly* 18:23–26.

Bunzel, Ruth, 1929. *The Pueblo Potter: A Study of Creative Imagination in Primitive Art*, Columbia University Contributions to Anthropology 8 (New York).

Bushnell, David I., Jr., 1906. The Sloane Collection in the British Museum. *American Anthropologist* 8:671–685.

Canaday, John, 1972a. Very Quiet and Very Dangerous. *New York Times*, Feb. 27, p. D21.

———, 1972b. A Few Last Words, Very Calm, About Selling the Public's Pictures. *New York Times*, March 19, p. D21.

Conklin, Harold C., and William C. Sturtevant, 1953. Seneca Indian Singing Tools at Coldspring Longhouse: Musical Instruments of the Modern Iroquois. *Proceedings of the American Philosophical Society* 97:262–290.

Cranstone, B. A. L., and H. J. Gowers, 1968. The Tahitian Mourner's Dress: A Discovery and a Description. *British Museum Quarterly* 32:138–144.

Dawson, Lawrence, and James Deetz, 1965. A Corpus of Chumash Basketry. Department of Anthropology, University of California, Los Angeles, *Archaeological Survey Annual Report 1965* (Los Angeles), pp. 197–212.

Deetz, James, 1968. Late Man in North America: Archeology of European Americans. In *Anthropological Archeology in the Americas*, Betty J. Meggers, ed. (Washington, D.C.: Anthropological Society of Washington), pp. 121–130.

Deetz, James A., and Edwin S. Dethlefson, 1965. The Doppler Effect and Archaeology: A Consideration of the Spatial Aspects of Seriation. *Southwestern Journal of Anthropology* 21:196–206.

———, 1967. Death's Head, Cherub, Urn and Willow. *Natural History* 76(3):28–27.

Dethlefson, Edwin, and James Deetz, 1966. Death's Heads, Cherubs, and Willow Trees: Experimental Archaeology in Colonial Cemeteries. *American Antiquity* 31:502–510.

Duff, Wilson, 1967. Charles Edenshaw: Master Artist. In *Arts of the Raven: Masterworks by the Northwest Coast Indian* (Vancouver: Vancouver Art Gallery).

Emery, Irene, 1966. *The Primary Structure of Fabrics: An Illustrated Classification* (Washington, D.C.: Textile Museum).

Faris, James C., 1972. *Nuba Personal Art* (London: Duckworth).

Feest, Christian F., 1968. *Review of* Indianer Nordamerikas 1760–1860 by H. Benndorf and A. Speyer. *Archiv für Völkerkunde* 22:144–147.

Fenton, William N., 1967. Field Work, Museum Studies, and Ethnohistorical Research. *Ethnohistory* 13:71–85.

Friedrich, Margaret Hardin, 1970. Design Structure and Social Interaction: Archaeological Implications of an Ethnographic Analysis. *American Antiquity* 35:332–343.

Gilborn, Craig, 1968. Pop Pedagogy: Looking at the Coke Bottle. *Museum News* 47(4):12–18.

Grew, Nehemiah, 1681. *Musaeum Regalis Societatis, or a Catalogue & Description of the Natural and Artificial Rarities Belonging to the Royal Society and Preserved at Gresham Colledge . . .* (London: Printed by W. Rawlins, for the author).

Hatt, Gudmund, 1916. *Moccasins and Their Relation to Arctic Footwear,* Memoirs of the American Anthropological Association No. 15 (Lancaster).

Hirschberg, Walter, Alfred Janata, Wilhelm P. Bauer, and Christian F. Feest, 1966. *Technologie und Ergologie in der Völkerkunde,* B · I Hochschultaschenbücher 338/338a/338b (Mannheim: Bibliographisches Institut).

Holm, Bill, 1965. *Northwest Coast Indian Art, an Analysis of Form* (Seattle: University of Washington Press).

Hunter, John E., 1967. *Inventory of Ethnological Collections in Museums of the United States and Canada,* 2nd ed. ([Milwaukee]: Milwaukee Public Museum).

Hymes, Dell, 1970. Linguistic Models in Archaeology. In *Archéologie et calculateurs: Problèmes sémiologiques et mathématiques* (Colloques internationaux du Centre nationale de la recherche scientifique, Sciences humaines, Marseilles, 7–12 avril 1969) (Paris: Editions du c.n.r.s.), pp. 91–118.

Kaemlein, Wilma R., 1967. *An Inventory of Southwestern American Indian Specimens in European Museums* (Tucson: Arizona State Museum).

Kaufmann, Carole N., 1969. Changes in Haida Indian Argillite Carving, 1820 to 1910. (Ph.D. diss., University of California, Los Angeles.)

Kidd, Kenneth E., and Martha Ann Kidd, 1970. A Classification System for Glass Beads for the Use of Field Archaeologists. *Canadian Historic Sites: Occasional Papers in Archaeology and History No. 1* (Ottawa), pp. 45–89.

Kluckhohn, Clyde, W. W. Hill, and Lucy Wales Kluckhohn, 1971. *Navaho Material Culture* (Cambridge: Belknap Press of Harvard University Press).

Koch, Gerd, 1961. *Die materielle Kultur der Ellice-Inseln,* Veröffentlichungen des Museums für Völkerkunde, Neue Folge 3, Abteilung Südsee 1 (Berlin).

———, 1965. *Materielle Kultur der Gilbert-Inseln: Nonouti, Tabiteuea, Onotoa,* Veröffentlichungen des Museums für Völkerkunde, Neue Folge 6, Abteilung Südsee 3 (Berlin).

———, 1971. *Materielle Kultur der Santa Cruz-Inseln, unter besonderer Berücksichtigung der Riff-Inseln.* Veröffentlichungen des Museums für Völkerkunde, Neue Folge 21, Abteilung Südsee 9 (Berlin).

Kubler, George, 1962. *The Shape of Time: Remarks on the History of Things* (New Haven: Yale University Press).

Lach, Donald F., 1970. *Asia in the Making of Europe*, vol. 2: *A Century of Wonder*, Book One: *The Visual Arts* (Chicago: University of Chicago Press). (Chap. 1: "Collections of Curiosities.")

LeBar, Frank M., 1964. *The Material Culture of Truk*, Yale University Publications in Anthropology No. 68 (New Haven).

Mason, Otis Tufton, 1904. Aboriginal American Basketry: Studies in a Textile Art without Machinery, *Report of the U.S. National Museum . . . for . . . 1902* (Washington, D.C.), pp. 171–548, 248 pls.

McGrath, Kyran M., 1970. The Official Museum Directory, United States—Canada 1971. ([No place]: American Association of Museums and Crowell-Collier Educational Corp.). (Geographically arranged; includes nearly all worthwhile North American museums, with address, telephone, hours, interests, some staff names; useful indexes at back. A new edition of this directory appears about every five years.)

Munn, Nancy D., 1962. Walbiri Graphic Signs: An Analysis. *American Anthropologist* 64:972–984.

———, 1966. Visual Categories: An Approach to the Study of Representational Systems *American Anthropologist* 68:936–950.

Museums Association [of Great Britain], 1971. *Museums Calendar, Including a Directory of Museums and Art Galleries of the British Isles Together with a Select List of Institutions Overseas* (London: The Museums Association). (An annual publication; the 1972 edition omits the useful "select list of institutions overseas.")

Newton, Dolores, 1971. Social and Historical Dimensions of Timbira Material Culture. (Ph.D. diss., Harvard University.)

O'Neale, Lila M., 1932. Yurok-Karok Basket Weavers, *University of California Publications in American Archaeology and Ethnology* 32(1):1–184 (Berkeley).

Ortiz, Fernando, 1952-1955. *Los instrumentos de la música afrocubana*, 5 vols. (Havana: Dirección de Cultura del Ministerio de Educación [y] Cárdenas y Cía).

Osgood, Cornelius, 1940. *Ingalik Material Culture*, Yale University Publications in Anthropology No. 22 (New Haven).

Rankin, Bunyan Kirk, III, 1965. A Linguistic Study of the Formation of Chinese Characters. (Ph.D. diss., University of Pennsylvania [University Microfilms 66–293].)

Ricciardelli, Alex F., 1967. A Census of Ethnological Collections in United States Museums. *Museum News* 46(1):11–14.

Rowe, John Howland, 1959. Archaeological Dating and Cultural Process. *Southwestern Journal of Anthropology* 15:317–324.

Sturtevant, William C., 1955. Osceola's Coats? *Florida Historical Quarterly* 34:315–328.

———, 1966. Ethnological Collections and Curatorial Records. *Museum News* 44(7):16–19.

———, 1967a. *Guide to Field Collecting of Ethnographic Specimens*. Smithsonian Institution Information Leaflet 503 (Washington, D.C.).

———, 1967b. Seminole Men's Clothing. *Proceedings of the 1966 Annual Spring Meeting of the American Ethnological Society* (Seattle), pp. 160–174.

———, 1969. Does Anthropology Need Museums? Pp. 619–649 in Papers Presented at a Symposium on Natural History Collections, Past, Present, Future, Daniel M. Cohen and Roger F. Cressey, eds., *Proceedings of the Biological Society of Washington* 82:559–762.

Tradescant, John, 1656. *Musaeum Tradescantianum: or, A Collection of Rarities Preserved at South-Lambeth neer London.* (London: Printed by John Grismond). (Reprinted in facsimile, except for the Garden List, as *Old Ashmolean Reprints* No. 1, Oxford, 1925.)

Watt, William C., 1966-1967. *Morphology of the Nevada Cattlebrands and Their Blazons*, Part One, National Bureau of Standards Report 9050 (NBS Project 205–205–2050404), (Washington, D.C.: U.S. Department of Commerce, 1966); Part Two, (Pittsburgh. Department of Computer Science, Carnegie-Mellon University, 1967).

———, 1967. Structural Properties of the Nevada Cattlebrands. *Computer Science Research Review* 2:21–27 (Pittsburgh: Computation Center and Department of Computer Science, Carnegie-Mellon University).

Woodbury, Nathalie F. S., ed., 1971. *Guide to Departments of Anthropology 1971–1972.* (Washington, D.C.: American Anthropological Association). (An annual publication. Museums with anthropologists on the staff are listed at the back, with the names and interests of the staff and some other data.)

Worm, Olaus, 1655. *Museum Wormianum, seu Historia rerum rariorum, tam naturalium, quam artificialium, tam domesticarum, quam exoticarum, quae Hafniae Danorum in aedibus authoris servantur* (Leiden: Ex Officina Elseviriorum, Acad. Typograph).

Careers for Archeologists in the National Park Service

GEORGE R. FISCHER

THE National Park Service offers a diversity of career opportunities for archeologists at all levels of academic training and experience. Some seventy archeologists are employed by the Service, approximately forty of whom are attached to the Division of Archeology and Anthropology. The remainder are employed by other units of the organization involved in planning, management, curatorial and museum work, interpretation of archeological areas for park visitors, and in other capacities which utilize their backgrounds as archeologists in functions other than research. The Service also employs a large number of temporary and part-time archeologists.

The basic responsibilities of the Service in archeology are derived from the Antiquities Act of 1906, which gives to the Secretary of the Interior responsibility for the protection of prehistoric and historic ruins, monuments, and objects situated on most federal lands. This responsibility has been delegated to the Director of the National Park Service.

In the Historic Sites Act of 1935, Congress declared, "It is a national policy to preserve for public use historic sites, buildings and objects of National significance." This act empowers "the Secretary of the Interior through the National Park Service" to effectuate this policy, and authorizes the Service to conduct surveys, publish studies, and otherwise encourage the preservation of historic properties not federally owned.

The Reservoir Salvage Act of 1960 provided specifically for the preservation of historic and archeological data that might otherwise be lost through dam construction.

In 1966 the responsibilities of the Service were expanded by the National Historic Preservation Act, which pledged federal assistance to preservation efforts undertaken by states and local governments and by the private sector. This act provided for an enlarged protective inventory of historic properties—the National Register—and established the Advisory Council on Historic Preservation to advise the President and the Congress on programs to enhance the nation's efforts in historic preservation.

To meet these responsibilities, the National Park Service administers a four-part program to recover and protect archeological remains. This program consists of: archeological investigations in areas of the National Park System where prehistoric and historic people have lived; investigation of archeological sites for the purpose of salvaging knowledge and evidence from them before they are flooded by federally sponsored water-control projects; preservation through stabilization of both prehistoric and historic ruins, earthworks, and building foundations revealed through archeology; publication of information derived from archeological investigations.

The National Park System contains one national park, Mesa Verde, in Colorado, and twenty national monuments set aside by the federal government because of their prehistoric archeological values. These archeological reserves are protected both so that visitors may appreciate the prehistoric cultures and research on them may continue. Additionally, among the more than two hundred and fifty other areas in the System set aside for scenic, recreational, or historical values, there exist highly significant resources. The nearly thirty million acres administered by the Service constitute one of the major reservoirs of protected archeological sites in this country. Research which has been conducted in the National Park System for scientific and management purposes constitutes an important source of the extant archeological data in the United States.

The archeological record of Europeans in the New World is an important component of our cultural heritage which, until relatively recently, received little attention from archeologists. Some one hundred and fifty units of the System preserve historical areas. Acquiring data on features of these areas and supplementing historical records have required the Service to develop a program in historic sites archeology. Following pioneer work nearly forty years ago at Jamestown National Historic Site, Virginia, the Service has been a leader in historic site investigations.

Many large areas in the United States are flooded by multipurpose dams on major rivers. Other land is trenched for oil and gas pipelines. Superhighways cut huge swaths across the countryside. In the paths of many of the projects lie archeological sites of major importance to our knowledge of the Indian past. The Service is responsible for the recovery of archeological remains in reservoir areas and other locations where construction activity threatens archeological and historical sites. It also coordinates research and allocates funds to qualified agencies and institutions which conduct the actual salvage work.

The Inter-Agency Archeological Salvage Program, sponsored by the National Park Service, constitutes a large proportion of the archeological fieldwork done in this country. It began after World War II when archeologists realized many sites were being inundated by reservoirs. Acting under the Antiquities Act of 1906, the Historic Sites Act of 1935, and the Reservoir Salvage Act of 1960, the National Park Service has developed a program to salvage archeological and historical materials and information in cooperation with local institutions and other government agencies.

As part of its responsibility to preserve the past, the National Park Service has developed a stabilization program for archeological sites. Through a variety of engineering and conservation techniques, stone or adobe forts and pueblos, earthworks, burial mounds, and brick foundations are stabilized to withstand the eroding effects of time and climate. The work is done in a manner that will alter the remains as little as possible.

Beyond learning from and protecting the places where archeology reveals the history of man, the National Park Service seeks to preserve and to share that knowledge. For this reason, the Service supports a program for the publication of information derived from archeological projects. The Archeological Research Series and Anthropological Series make such knowledge widely available in the form of published reports used in libraries and research institutions. Additionally, reports and monographs of specific interest are reproduced in limited and less formal format for distribution to scholars and institutions interested in particular, specialized research areas.

The Washington office of the Division of Archeology and Anthropology serves primarily a management function. The archeological programs of the Service operate from four archeological centers in Tallahassee, Florida; Lincoln, Nebraska; the University of New Mexico campus at Albuquerque; and the University of Arizona campus at Tucson. Field offices also operate in Philadelphia, San Francisco, Seattle, and Alaska. Permanent bases are maintained at major excavation sites during the periods of specific projects. As part of its role as advisor on archeological problems for eighteen federal land-managing agencies, the Service has archeologists on assignment to the Bureau of Land Management and Bureau of Indian Affairs.

As the concept of National Parks was originated in the United States, and has, in most cases, only recently been developed by other countries, the Service is frequently called upon for advice and assistance by foreign nations. Teams of park experts, including archeologists, have been sent on special assignments abroad on many occasions. Assistance to other countries has recently been given to Jordan, Turkey, Peru, and Guatemala.

Current major research projects of the Service include excavations at Fort Vancouver National Historic Site, Washington, the site of the western headquarters of the Hudson's Bay Company in 1825 and a United States military reservation for one hundred years thereafter; and Fort Stanwix National Monument, Rome, New York, a Revolutionary War site historically significant in having repulsed the British invasion from Canada. Among several areas of basic research are identification of mammal bones from archeological sites, underwater archeology, and archeological survey by remote sensing techniques.

As one of the purposes of this paper is to apprise archeologists of a significant but poorly known source of employment, a brief description follows of the types of employment opportunities available, qualifications required, and the processes of application.

Many opportunities exist for seasonal or temporary positions in the Service. The majority of these are in archeological areas of the system and involve interpretation of park features to visitors. The interpretive personnel are required to wear the uniform of the National Park Service. Minimum qualifications are that the applicant must be at least eighteen years of age and have any combination of education beyond high school or qualifying experience totaling two years. The Service's purpose for hiring seasonal, uniformed employees is twofold; first, to augment the permanent staff during the periods of peak activity, and second, to introduce young people having interest in possible career employment to the professional opportunities available. The initial grade level for these positions is GS–4. Application should be made to the superintendent of the archeological area in which employment is desired (see Appendix A). The standard "Application for Federal Employment" form should be used, and may be obtained at most post offices or the personnel office of any federal agency.

Opportunities exist for temporary employment within the Division of Archeology and Anthropology as members of field crews, in curatorial or laboratory work, in ruins stabilization, or in other areas of research. Because the work is often at a semi- or subprofessional level, hiring is frequently done locally. To be considered for this type of employment, the standard application form should be sent to the field offices themselves (see Appendix B).

Permanent appointments to the Service may be obtained at all grade levels. Most archeologists enter the Service shortly after completion of their education. The basic entrance level qualifications for grade GS–5 are: a B.A. from a college or university with a strong background in anthropology, or twenty semester hours of college anthropology courses plus experience equal to a four-year education. Three months of archeological excavation experience under the direction of a recognized professional archeologist is also required. Qualifying for grade GS–7 requires a minimum of one year of professional experience, one year of graduate study in anthropology, or a combination of experience and education totaling one year. Superior academic achievement or high scores on the Federal Service Entrance Examination or Graduate Record Examination will also qualify candidates for the higher grade. Initially these positions are in interpretive work. Qualified individuals may later transfer into the research arm of the Service.

Archeologists with higher degrees and more extensive experience may enter at any of the higher grade levels, depending upon their qualifications, and be assigned directly to one of the research activities. Information on mid-level and senior level appointments may be obtained through the U.S. Civil Service Commission, Washington, D.C. 20415. Specific information on the opportunities available to more highly qualified individuals may be obtained by writing to the Division of Archeology and Anthropology, National Park Service, Washington, D.C. 20240.

Appendix A

NATIONAL PARK SERVICE ARCHEOLOGICAL AREAS

Aztec Ruins National Monument, Route 1, Box 101, Aztec, New Mexico 87410

Bandelier National Monument, Los Alamos, New Mexico 87544

Canyon de Chelly National Monument, Box 588, Chinle, Arizona 86503

Casa Grande Ruins National Monument, Box 518, Coolidge, Arizona 85228

Chaco Canyon National Monument, Star Route, Bloomfield, New Mexico 87413

Effigy Mounds National Monument, Box K, McGregor, Iowa 52157

Gila Cliff Dwellings National Monument, Gila Hot Springs, New Mexico 88061

Gran Quivira National Monument, Route 1, Mountainair, New Mexico 87036

Hovenweep National Monument, c/o Mesa Verde National Park, Mesa Verde National Park, Colorado 81330

Mesa Verde National Park, Mesa Verde National Park, Colorado 81330

Montezuma Castle National Monument, Box 218, Camp Verde, Arizona 86322

Mound City Group National Monument, Box 327, Chillicothe, Ohio 45601

Navajo National Monument, Tonalea, Arizona 86044

Ocmulgee National Monument, Box 4186, Macon, Georgia 31208

Pecos National Monument, Drawer 11, Pecos, New Mexico 87552

Pipestone National Monument, Box 727, Pipestone, Minnesota 56164

Russell Cave National Monument, Bridgeport, Alabama 35740

Tonto National Monument, Box 707, Roosevelt, Arizona 85445

Tuzigoot National Monument, Box 68, Clarkdale, Arizona 86324

Walnut Canyon National Monument, Route 1, Box 790, Flagstaff, Arizona 86001

Wupatki National Monument, Tuba Star Route, Flagstaff, Arizona 86001

Appendix B

NATIONAL PARK SERVICE REGIONAL OFFICES

National Capitol Parks
National Park Service
1100 Ohio Drive, s.w.
Washington, D.C. 20242
Administering National Park Service Operations in
Washington, D.C., metropolitan area

Northeast Region
National Park Service
143 South Third Street
Philadelphia, Pennsylvania 19106
Administering National Park Service Operations in
Connecticut, Delaware, Illinois, Indiana, Maine, Maryland, Massachusetts, Michigan, Minnesota, New Hampshire, New Jersey, New York, Ohio, Pennsylvania, Rhode Island, Vermont, Virginia, West Virginia, and Wisconsin

Southeast Region
National Park Service
Federal Building, Box 10008
400 North Eighth Street
Richmond, Virginia 23204
Administering National Park Service Operations in
Alabama, Florida, Georgia, Kentucky, Mississippi, North Carolina, South Carolina, Tennessee, Puerto Rico, and the Virgin Islands

Midwest Region
National Park Service
1709 Jackson Street
Omaha, Nebraska 68102

Administering National Park Service Operations in
Colorado, Iowa, Kansas, Missouri, Montana, Nebraska, North Dakota, South Dakota, Utah, and Wyoming

Southwest Region
National Park Service
Old Santa Fe Trail
P. O. Box 728
Santa Fe, New Mexico 87501

Administering National Park Service Operations in
Arkansas, Louisiana, New Mexico, Oklahoma, and Texas

Northwest Region
National Park Service
Room 931, 4th and Pike Building
Seattle, Washington 98101

Administering National Park Service Operations in
Alaska, Idaho, Oregon, and Washington

Western Region
National Park Service
450 Golden Gate Avenue
Box 36063
San Francisco, California 94102

Administering National Park Service Operations in
Arizona, California, Hawaii, and Nevada

Anthropology in Schools

WILFRID C. BAILEY

A Kazak's house is called a yurt,
Called a yurt,
Called a yurt.
A Kazak's house is called a yurt. A yurt?!
A yurt's a kind of tent.

A yurt is made of wood and felt,
Wood and felt,
Wood and felt.
A yurt is made of wood and felt. Of felt?!
Felt is a kind of wool.

The Kazak moves his yurt by yak,
Yurt by yak,
Yurt by yak.
The Kazak moves his yurt by yak. By yak?!
A yak's a mountain ox.

—"The Kazak's House"
by Jean Blackwood
(Hunt, Blackwood, and Emmons, 1968:32)

THE ABOVE has been sung to the tune of "Here We Go Round the Mulberry Bush" by children between the ages of four and six as they learned about the concept of culture. The last word in each stanza was one of the words they talked about in their discussion of Kazak culture. Yes, the concept of culture can be and has been taught to preschool children (Hunt 1969). Thousands of students in grades K through 12 have been exposed to anthropology.

For much of its history, anthropology has been associated with museums and universities. Most students have known nothing about it until they reached college, and then it was usually by accident that they stumbled into the introductory course. In the future, college teachers will discover that more and more students in their classes have some prior knowledge about anthropology.

Anthropology has reached a new high in the awareness of the public. Margaret Mead is a familiar figure to a large segment of the American public. As the high priestess of anthropology, she has appeared on TV as a participant in Congressional hearings, has seized the speaking platform from presidential candidates, and has been a frequent contributor to women's magazines (Mead and Metraux 1970). At the same time anthropology has reached into the schools. The receptiveness of primary and secondary level schools is, to a large extent, directly related to public awareness of the nature of anthropology and a comprehension of its possible contribution to understanding the world today.

Anthropology has invaded the schools in three ways. First, anthropology has assumed an important role in teacher education, either through regular courses in anthropology departments or courses with anthropological content taught in what are sometimes called departments of social foundations of education. Books of readings for the latter increasingly contain articles related to anthropology (Lindquest 1970; Chilcott, Greenberg, and Wilson 1968). A variety of books has appeared that present anthropology to the teacher. They have been written by both anthropologists and others (Pelto 1965; Kneller 1965). Walter Goldschmidt prepared a pamphlet to assist teachers with students considering going into anthropology (1970). Second, anthropologists and others utilizing anthropological techniques have been studying educational systems and classrooms as structures for the process of cultural transmission (Burnett 1969; Brameld 1968). Third, a variety of curriculum materials has been developed to facilitate the teaching of anthropology at a variety of grade levels. This paper is concerned with the curriculum aspect of anthropology in the schools.

It is difficult to say when anthropology was first introduced into the classroom. Except for history and geography, the various social sciences have been lumped together under a single umbrella, social studies. The result has been an interdisciplinary approach in which the various subjects treating human relations lost their identity. However, anthropological materials were utilized in a variety of ways.

The opening chapters in world history texts usually start with a discussion of human origins and periods before the dawn of civilization. American histories include a section on the American Indian. Unfortunately, these chapters are almost uniformly either simple-minded pap or grossly inaccurate. An examination of a series of world history textbooks revealed that, besides material of questionable accuracy, they made little or no use of anthropological concepts such as culture, culture change, and diffusion. Culture change usually was equated with progress or advancement.

> Man was first a savage, then a barbarian, and finally a civilized being. The *savage* depends almost entirely on nature. He secures food from wild plants and wild animals; he knows nothing of metals but makes his tools and weapons of stone, wood, and bone; he wears little or no clothing; his home is merely a cave, a rock shelter, or a hut of bark. Such primitive folk still live in the interior of Africa and Australia. The *barbarian* has gained more control over nature than the savage. He plants seeds, has domesticated animals and uses some metal implements. Most of the American Indians before the coming of Columbus and most of the Negroes in Africa may be classified as barbarians. (Heath "Record of Mankind," quoted by Mayer 1962:116)

Some of the geography textbooks are more palatable to anthropologists. Atwood and Thomas (1943) produced an elementary school world geography that takes the students on "imaginary visits with children in widely scattered parts of the world" and strives, as one of its purposes, "to demonstrate the fact that adaptation to conditions of physical environment imposed by nature underlies the life of all peoples, from those of the most primitive cultures to the most advanced" (iii). Here Dick and Jane are replaced by Bunga, the Malaya Nigrito; Netsook and Klaya, Eskimo; Iuvan, Kazak; and Simba, in the Congo. The content is rather good. Perhaps, the best example from geography books is Sauer's *Man in Nature: A First Book in Geography* (1939), that uses Wissler's culture areas of North America to illustrate man's adjustment to geographical or natural areas.

Numerous school systems have required units on American Indians. Unfortunately, these often never got beyond wigwams and papooses that reinforced popular stereotypes. The Pennsylvania schools were required by the state legislature to teach "World Cultures." This author attended a planning session in Harrisburg in 1964, along with representatives of various anthropology curriculum projects, to assist in injecting anthropological concepts in the unit design. Almost nothing in systematic anthropology was attempted below the ninth grade. Only a handful of high schools had tried courses in anthropology prior to 1960. These included Verde Valley in Sedonia, Arizona. Clyde Kluckhohn was one of the founders of this unusual private school that included anthropology as a major element in its curriculum. Other schools were Edsel Ford in Dearborn, Germantown Friends in Philadelphia, and Columbus in Indiana (Mayer 1962:115–116).

Educators at many levels were very much aware of the increasing importance of anthropology as a discipline and its potential contribution. World War II and the foreign aid programs that followed clearly demonstrated the need for the understanding of cultures that could result from the use of anthropological materials. Even the state of Georgia authorized a high school level course in cultural anthropology and recommended the incorporation of anthropological materials in elementary school social studies. However, there was one very important roadblock in incorporating into the curriculum the rapidly expanding discipline of anthropology. There was an appalling lack of good materials that could be used in the classroom. In addition, very few classroom teachers and school administrators had taken even one anthropology course in their teacher training programs. Two of the earliest books on anthropology suitable for high school use were *People and Places* by Margaret Mead (1959) and *Four Ways of Being Human* by Gene Lisitsky (1956). The latter was neither an anthropologist nor an educator. Neither book was a systematic presentation of anthropological concepts. Both were comparative ethnologies.

October 4, 1957, the date that the Soviet Union launched the world's first man-made satellite, Sputnik I, opened up a new era in American education. Americans feared that the United States was being surpassed technologically and culturally by the Russians. Attention was directed to the schools as the ultimate reason for the lack of progress. The immediate concern was to beef up the science courses from the elementary grades on up. Soon, efforts to improve the curriculum broadened to include the social sciences and the humanities. The development of the new curriculum was supported first by the National Science Foundation. The most influential step in the social studies was taken by the United States Office of Education when it kicked off its Project Social Studies. New curriculum efforts were also aided and abetted by textbook publishers anxious to capture the market swelled by a rapidly growing school population.

Curriculum writing projects were started at both the top and the bottom in the educational system. A few were rather large projects financed by federal funds, and hundreds were in-shop activities carried out by individual school systems at either the local or the state level. Even in the latter, the source of funding was through the various national education acts. One important innovation was to utilize professionals from the various social sciences as consultants or even as project staff.

Three general approaches have been used in organizing the new curriculum. The most popular design has been multidisciplinary, incorporating the basic concepts and methods of the individual disciplines. One of the most widely known multidisciplinary curriculums has been the expanding communities promoted by Paul R. Hanna of Stanford University. It begins in the first grade with the child's own family and moves out through the community, state, region, and nation in later grades. Hanna asks the students to think and to investigate problems from the standpoint of a historian, political scientist, human geographer, sociologist, economist, and anthropologist (Hanna, Kohn, and Steeg 1970; Hanna 1963).

The second type of curriculum utilizes anthropology in special purposes units. These can be classified into two categories. One emphasizes teaching strategy (Taba 1967). The other utilizes anthropology, particularly the concept of culture, in materials for teaching languages, history, geography, etc.

The third type of curriculum employs single discipline or partial programs. The units are based on a single social science such as political science, economics, sociology, or anthropology. They have been labeled "partial programs" because they are designed to be used as a segment in or a supplement to the overall curriculum and are not expected to be an entire social studies program (Thomas and Brubaker 1971:219). Several of these projects focused on anthropology.

The net result of these approaches and the multiplicity of projects has been a hodge-podge of units. Not all disciplines are available for every grade. There are many blanks and much overlapping. Probably another round of curriculum development will follow, systematically utilizing the results of experimental units. We can hope that the new material will have a sound scientific basis.

Before 1960 very few high schools taught anthropology. Scattered pioneers did try teaching units or even courses in anthropology. Most were forced to improvise materials from professional monographs or college-level texts. For example, one Chicago high school employed Margaret Mead's *Cultural Patterns and Technical Change* (Mead 1953; Warren 1963). It was not until recently that high school-level textbooks in general anthropology appeared (Cover 1971; Salzmann 1969).

The first major project to produce curriculum materials for the high school level was the Anthropology Curriculum Study Project directed by Mrs. Malcolm Collier. This project began in 1962 and concluded in 1971 (Collier 1972). It was financed by grants totaling about $1,250,000 from the National Science Foundation (NSF) to the American Anthropological Association. A long process of experimenting and testing resulted in a series known as *Patterns of Human History* published by the Macmillan Company. The four units, *Studying Societies, Origins of Humanness, The Emergence of Complex Societies*, and *Modernization and Traditional Societies*, were designed for use in the first semester of a world history course. *Studying Societies* is basic, and the other parts can be added if desired. The four together could be the basis of a separate high school course in anthropology. In addition to student readings and guides, the units contain records, film strips, overhead transparencies, evidence cards, and artifact casts. These lend themselves to deductive or discovery teaching techniques. An outgrowth of the Anthropology Curriculum Study Project was the Anthropology Case Materials Project at Indiana University, funded by NSF and directed by Robert G. Hanvey.

Several high school classes have been introduced to anthropology through actual participation in archeological excavation. A decade ago, students at Sedro Valley High School, Washington, climaxed a course in anthropology by assisting a University of Washington field team in excavating a site (Dunlap 1961). Students from the anthropology class at Fenster Ranch School in Tucson carried on excavations under the direction of their teacher, but supervised by the Arizona State Museum (Zahniser 1966). The same teacher has since used high school students on Santa Catalina Island, California, and at Rancho de Taos, New Mexico.

The construction of Pebblebrook High School, Mableton, Georgia, partially destroyed an archeological site. A local amateur arranged for salvage archeology of the remaining portions of the site. Digging was done by high school students on released time from class. Direct supervision was given by Dr. Arthur R. Kelly, professor emeritus, University of Georgia, and classroom instruction was assisted by Marilyn Pennington, a graduate student at the University of Georgia. The project had a broad, sweeping impact when the enthusiasm of the students caught the adults in the community, and they became concerned about the fate of other archeological sites in the area affected by urban growth. As a result of this interest, a survey of archeological sites, both prehistoric and historic, was conducted during the summer of 1970. A total of 133 sites were surveyed, 42 of these previously unknown. At the present time, excavation has begun at another site and a second high school has become involved.

Several projects have developed curriculum units for the elementary grades. *Man: A Course of Study* was produced by the Educational Development Center, Cambridge, Massachusetts. This fifth-grade unit consists of twenty-three booklets, games, pictures, recordings, slides, and films. It progresses from the study of salmon and baboons to the Netsilik Eskimo. The movies on the baboons are the work of Irvin Devore, and those on the Netsilik by Asen Balikci are now widely known (Balikci and Brown 1966). A major drawback on use of these materials is their high cost. In addition, teachers are required to attend a special workshop.

In 1964 the United States Office of Education funded the Anthropology Curriculum Project at the University of Georgia. This experimental program developed a graded sequence of units for kindergarten through grade 7 plus five additional units for the junior high school level. The project has been under the direction of Marion J. Rice, College of Education, and Wilfrid C. Bailey, Department of Sociology and Anthropology. The project was based on the proposition that anthropology had a framework of concepts that could be learned by elementary school children (Rice and Bailey 1971).

The first step in the project was to survey the field of anthropology to determine its content, basic concepts, and contributions. This was done by analyzing twenty-nine introductory anthropology textbooks. The examination of the texts revealed remarkably little agreement on core concepts or theory. However, a list of basic concepts associated with the several branches of anthropology was developed and then evaluated with six consultants representing different fields of anthropology. The basic concepts were arranged in a spiral curriculum. That is, major concepts were repeated at two levels. The sequence begins with units on the *Concept of Culture* at grades 1 and 4. *The Development of Man and His Culture* includes *New World Prehistory* for grade 2 and *Old World Prehistory* and *Human Evolution* for grade 5. *Culture Change* is the topic for grades 3 and 6. A second series of units were developed for the junior high level. They include *Language, Life Cycle, Political Anthropology, The Urban Community*, and *Race, Caste, and Prejudice*. In addition, the first grade unit on the *Concept of Culture* was rewritten for use at the kindergarten level.

Pupils are exposed to more than a series of anthropological concepts and topics. Each unit includes case studies representing various world culture areas. The *Concept of Culture* uses Arunta, Kazak, and modern America. *Life Cycle* includes China, Tiv, the Balkan peasant, and modern America. *Culture Change* utilizes material from Mexico, India, Japan, Africa, and modern America. Thus, students are able to look at a series of cultures, including their own.

Four questions can be asked concerning the introduction of anthropology into classrooms below the college level. What has been its reception? Can teachers effectively use anthropological materials? Can the children learn anthropology? What of the future?

The great volume of articles in educational publications and the vast number of papers presented at educational meetings indicate a high level of interest. All projects have been deluged with inquiries. The Georgia project can serve as an example. From June 1964 through September 1970, a total of 3,357 requests for information were received. In the same period, 5,172 sample sets and 594 classroom sets were sold. Income from sales has made it possible for the project to continue since the termination of federal funding in 1969. Northern and far western states have shown more interest than southern and plains states.

The range of reception is illustrated in letters received in response to an article that appeared in an educational publication, *The Instructor* (Bailey and Clune 1965).

> I never knew what anthropology was. I don't know what anthropology is. I don't care what anthropology is. I don't intend to be told what anthropology is. Get the message?
>
> Disgusted

I enjoyed the anthropology article very much. . . . Let's have more of this approach. . . . It's really worthwhile.

Indiana

On a more serious note, there have been several objections to anthropological units. One objection has been to the unfamiliar vocabulary and concepts. Observation suggests that teachers were more concerned than the students. The most common objection, and the one most feared by teachers and administrators, was to the inclusion of human evolution. One school immediately withdrew from the experimental testing program. In another case, where the fifth-grade unit was adopted for use in a high school science class, it was one of the factors contributing to the resignation of the principal. The new administrator forced the teacher to seek a new school for the next year. Not only did he drop the unit out of the curriculum, but he also withdrew from the library all of the books on anthropology.

Objections to evolution were not limited to the Bible Belt South. The most vigorous personal attack on this author occurred in Seattle, Washington. A student assistant on the project wrote a thesis based on a survey of teachers using the unit in the Georgia experimental schools. He compared the teachers on their knowledge of the concept of evolution and the degree to which they felt that the concept of evolution conflicted with their personal belief system. The results showed that the two were inversely related. Teachers who felt the greatest conflict had the least knowledge of evolution, whereas those who knew the most about evolution experienced the least conflict (Schneider 1966).

Can school teachers effectively teach anthropology? Teachers, especially those in the lower grades, must be generalists and are called upon to teach the whole range of material in the total curriculum. They cannot be expected to be specialists in all fields. Furthermore, relatively few teachers have taken formal courses in anthropology. Therefore, the acceptance of anthropology units depends on their usability by any qualified teacher. Many of the projects have involved teacher-training programs. In some cases this was mandatory.

The Anthropology Curriculum Study Project conducted an extensive test of the teachability of its material. *Patterns of Human History* was taught in two California cities by twenty-six teachers in eight high schools to thirteen hundred students.

The question of teacher training influenced the design of the units produced by the Georgia Anthropology Curriculum Project. Each unit was self-contained. That is, it included teacher background materials and teacher guides that were based on the assumption that the teacher had no prior knowledge of anthropology. In order to examine the degree to which self-sufficiency was achieved, the cooperation of a number of schools in Georgia was obtained. Two groups of teachers from each school participated in field testing the units. Teachers in an experimental group attended summer institutes in anthropology at the University of Georgia. A control group of teachers from the same schools as the experimental group did not receive the special training in anthropology.

Gains made by pupils taught by the two groups of teachers were compared. The difference between the achievement made by the pupils of trained teachers and the pupils of the teachers not receiving special training was not significant. Correlations between pupils' gains in anthropology and the teachers' grades in anthropology were not significant. Level of certification and age of the teacher were the significant sources of variance. This seemed to demonstrate that a teacher with ordinary training could successfully teach the units (Greene 1966).

Can children learn anthropology? The underlying philosophy of post-Sputnik curriculum development has been that children can learn anything presented in the form of concepts stated at a level they can understand. Anthropology has provided another test of this proposition. Testimonials from teachers and pupils are not enough. The testing programs of the Anthropology Curriculum Study Project at the high school level and the Anthropology Curriculum Project at the elementary school level clearly demonstrate that pupils can learn the material. None of the standard tests used in the schools were found to measure knowledge of anthropology. Both projects were forced to develop instruments that test the content of their units. The usual design was a pretest given before the start of the unit followed by one or more post-tests given during and at the close of the unit. The results demonstrated that pupils did make significant gains. This was true from the high school level on down, including kindergarten (Hunt 1969). However, the impact of their exposure to anthropology is not clear. One year-long high school course on world cultures seemed to reduce ethnocentrism, but did not increase ability to think critically about social problems (Lalor 1966). A short unit on race and prejudice did not clearly support the hypothesis that increased knowledge reduces negative attitudes between racial groups (Kleg 1970).

What of the future? The emphasis is no longer on projects to develop curriculums for the separate disciplines. Foundation money has shifted to other things. It is questionable whether the units prepared by these projects will see general adoption. Timing was bad. Because of complications involved in commercial publishing when federal funds are used, the distribution of the materials was frequently restricted. By the time they were ready for release, the interest of the educational public had shifted.

Probably the greatest impact of the anthropology project will be stimulation of interest in anthropology. Colleges of education now require more academic courses. For example, social studies education majors at the University of Georgia now take more substantive courses in the social sciences than social science majors in the College of Arts and Sciences. Many states now permit certification of teachers in anthropology. Some high schools are moving to a twelve-month plan with four quarters. This arrangement will require a move in the direction of courses that are a single quarter in length. Students will take more courses and it will be less difficult to work a course in anthropology into the schedule.

The great need for the future will be for continued input by anthropologists into the system. Much of this will have to be in an advisory capacity. Anthropologists will have to become involved in evaluation of anthropologically related areas of textbooks. There are hundreds of books on peoples of the world that have been written for school children. They, too, need to be evaluated. *Natural History* and many educational publications run reviews. The National Council of the Social Studies is bringing out a *Guide to Reading for Social Studies Teachers* (Bailey 1972). James J. Gallagher produced *An Annotated Bibliography of Anthropological Materials for High School Use* (1967).

One point is clear. Thousands of school children are hearing of anthropology. This is already being reflected in the enrollment in introductory anthropology courses. The introduction of anthropological content into the classroom below the college level will have an impact on public attitudes and on the university.

REFERENCES

Atwood, Wallace W., and Hellen Goss Thomas, 1943. *Visits in Other Lands* (Boston: Ginn).

Bailey, Wilfrid C., 1972. Anthropology. In *Guide to Reading for Social Science Teachers*, Jonathon C. McLendon, ed. (Washington, D.C.: National Council for the Social Studies).

Bailey, Wilfrid C., and Francis J. Clune, 1965. Anthropology for Elementary Schools. *The Instructor* 75:48–50.

Balikci, Asen, and Quentin Brown, 1966. *Ethnographic Filming and the Netsilik Eskimo* (Newton, Mass.: Educational Services).

Brameld, Theodore, 1968. *Japan: Culture, Education, and Change in Two Communities* (New York: Holt, Rinehart and Winston).

Burnett, Jacquetta H., 1969. Ceremony, Rites, and Economy in the Student System of an American High School. *Human Organization* 28:1–10.

Chilcott, John H., Norman C. Greenberg, and Herbert B. Wilson, 1968. *Readings in the Socio-cultural Foundations of Education* (Belmont, Calif.: Wadsworth).

Collier, Malcolm, ed., 1972. *Two-way Mirror: Anthropologists and Educators Observe Themselves and Each Other.* (Washington, D.C.: American Anthropological Association).

Cover, Lois B., 1971. *Anthropology for Our Times* (New York: Oxford Book).

Dunlap, Robert L., 1961. Teaching Anthropology in High School. *Washington Education* 72:16–18.

Gallagher, James J., 1967. *An Annotated Bibliography of Anthropological Materials for High School Use* (New York: Macmillan).

Goldschmidt, Walter, 1970. *On Becoming an Anthropologist* (Washington, D.C.: American Anthropological Association).

Greene, William W., Jr., 1966. Anthropological Teaching in the First and Fourth Grades: A Comparison of Trained and Non-trained Teachers as Measured by Pupil Performance. (Ed.D. diss., University of Georgia.)

Hanna, Paul R., 1963. Revising the Social Studies: What Is Needed? *Social Organization* 27:192–195.

Hanna, Paul R., Clyde F. Kohn, and Clarence L. Ver Steeg, 1970. *Investigating Man's World: Regional Studies* (Glenview, Ill.: Scott, Foresman).

Hunt, Anne, 1969. Anthropology Achievement in the Kindergarten. (Ed.D. diss., University of Georgia.)

Hunt, Anne, Jean Blackwood, and Frances Emmons, 1968. *Concept of Culture: An Introductory Unit*, Anthropology Curriculum Project and Development Center in Educational Stimulation Publication, No. 51 (Athens, Ga.).

Kleg, Milton, 1970. *Race, Caste, and Prejudice: The Influence of Change in Knowledge on Change in Attitude.* (Ed.D. diss., University of Georgia.)

Kneller, George F., 1965. *Educational Anthropology: An Introduction* (New York: John Wiley and Sons).

Lalor, Ida B., 1966. Insights Gained as a Result of a High School Social Studies Course. (Ph.D. diss., University of Chicago.)

Lindquest, Harry M., 1970. *Education: Readings in the Process of Cultural Transmission* (Boston: Houghton Mifflin).

Lisitzky, Gene, 1956. *Four Ways of Being Human: An Introduction to Anthropology* (New York: Viking Press).

Mayer, Martin, 1962. *Social Studies in American Schools* (New York: Harper and Row).

Mead, Margaret, 1953. *Cultural Patterns and Technical Change* (Paris: United Nations Educational, Scientific and Cultural Organization).

———, 1959. *People and Places* (New York: World).

Mead, Margaret, and Rhoda Metraux, 1970. *A Way of Seeing* (New York: McCall).

Pelto, Pertti J., 1965. *The Study of Anthropology* (Columbus, Ohio: Charles E. Merrill).

Rice, Marion J., and Wilfrid C. Bailey, 1971. *The Development of a Sequential Curriculum in Anthropology, Grades 1–7: Final Report* (Athens, Ga.: Anthropology Curriculum Project).

Salzmann, Zdenek, 1969. *Anthropology* (New York: Harcourt, Brace and World).

Sauer, Carl, 1939. *Man in Nature: A First Book in Geography* (New York: Charles Scribner's Sons).

Schneider, Kent A., 1966. Selected Correlates of Religious Involvement and Their Implication for Teaching Scientific Materials. (M.A. thesis, University of Georgia.)

Taba, Hilda, 1967. *Teacher's Handbook for Elementary Social Studies* (Reading, Mass.: Addison-Wesley).

Thomas, R. Murray and Dale L. Brubaker, 1971. *Curriculum Patterns in Elementary Social Studies* (Belmont, Calif.: Wadsworth).

Warren, Richard L., 1963. Anthropology and the Social Studies. *California Social Science Review* 3:10–16.

Zahniser, Jack L., 1966. A Didactic Postscript. *The Kiva* 31:192–200.

Education in Micronesia and Alaska: The Problems of Change

JAMES HAWKINS

SUPERFICIALLY, there would seem to be few more disparate places than Micronesia and Alaska. Lightly clothed, barefooted Micronesians on scattered, sun-splashed islands in a tropic sea contrast dramatically with fur-clad Eskimos inhabiting the desolate reaches of the Arctic tundra. Beneath these surface differences, however, lie amazing similarities between Arctic and western Alaska and the Pacific Islands of Micronesia.

Micronesia (the Trust Territory of the Pacific Islands) is a group of some two thousand islands in the far western Pacific. The islands begin six hundred miles east of the Philippines and are strung in a broad band just north of the equator three thousand miles toward Hawaii. They include the Mariana, the Caroline, and the Marshall Islands, and during World War II were famous for such names as Saipan, Peleliu, Kwajalien, and Truk—the scene of some of the most bitterly contested battles of the war. Since then the islands have been administered by the United States under a United Nations Trusteeship Agreement which required the administering authority to train the islanders for "independence or self government." Only ninety-six of the islands are inhabited, the population totaling slightly less than a hundred thousand. There are few resources, and many of the islands separating the great distances of ocean make transportation and communication difficult.

With these basic facts one begins to see a similarity between Arctic and western Alaska, and Micronesia. In both areas the native people are living on the fringes of Western culture and are seeking to penetrate the twentieth century. In both, there is a subsistence economy and little opportunity for dollar employment. In both areas great distances separate small communities, making transportation and communication difficult. A diversity of native cultures characterizes both areas and most children come to school speaking a different language than English. In both places an American administration is seeking to bring the native people into the twentieth century as active participants in a changing world. In both areas the traditional cultures are undergoing change and deterioration.

The educational systems of Alaska and Micronesia offer some interesting contrasts. The program of education for Alaskan natives follows traditional United States schooling. In almost every instance the teachers are Caucasian, have been trained in fully accredited institutions, hold at least a bachelor's degree, and are certified to teach in American elementary or secondary schools. The school buildings, usually modern, bear little resemblance to the homes of the village in which they are located. The objectives of education in Arctic and western Alaska are to permit the child to move fully into American life and to participate in the American economic system. The Alaskan native does not control his own educational system and has little voice in the educational decisions being made for him.

In Micronesia, on the other hand, most of the teachers in the elementary schools and at least half of the teachers in the secondary schools are Micronesians. Few have attended a college or university and almost none are certified in the American meaning of the word. The schools themselves, frequently of local manufacture with local materials, while picturesque, are not ideally suited for educational purposes. They frequently lack professional supervision, and the language of instruction for most elementary schools is not English. Text books and educational materials are inadequate. A major similarity with Alaska, however, is the establishment of boarding high schools as the major post-elementary educational component.

Some clear historical reasons account for the differences in the educational programs in Alaska and Micronesia. American education came early to Alaska with never any question that Alaska, as part of the United States, would some day fulfill its destiny as a state of the Union. Hence, those charged with making educational policies modeled the Alaskan system of education after that found in the continental United States. This required, among other things, using American text books, certified teachers, and a curriculum that would permit graduates to move into American society. For many years the educational policy-makers paid little attention to the problems posed by children who speak a different language and represent a different culture attempting to succeed in an American system.

Micronesia has a history of domination by a succession of major world powers. Spain controlled the area until 1900 when Germany purchased the islands to add to its Pacific empire. At the beginning of World War I Japan occupied the islands and continued to dominate the area until the last days of World War II, when the United States took the islands in a series of naval engagements and invasions. Since 1946 the United States' attitudes and policies have dominated.

During the early years of the United States trusteeship, responsible educational development lagged. Congressional appropriations were low and it was clear that, if education was to be achieved, a major effort had to be made by Micronesia. As a result, teachers were trained in local training institutions with assistance from American supervisors and teacher trainers. Local and district school boards were established and local taxes collected to pay the salaries of Micronesian teachers.

At that time the objective of education in the islands was to produce a Micronesian competent to deal with the island environment in order to improve his subsistence economy. Better methods of agricultural production were taught, as well as improved sanitation and health procedures. Few children went beyond the sixth grade, although intermediate schools through the equivalent of grade 9 were located in six larger communities. One secondary school served the population, enrolling not more than two hundred of the most highly qualified youth. The secondary school, taught in English, prepared its graduates for possible further work in medicine, education, and public administration.

In 1962 a radical change began to occur in Micronesian education. The American administration decided to accelerate Micronesian development and improve the educational system for the islands. This policy change greatly increased the educational budget, brought in large numbers of well qualified American teachers, improved the quantity and quality of textbooks and educational materials, and instigated construction of modern school buildings. Micronesians lost control of their educational system. Initially, little thought was given to the special problems posed by language and cultural differences. The difficulties inherent in this policy became apparent to the administration after several years and modifications began to take place. Language was the first educational problem to receive major consideration. A special curriculum was developed to teach English as a second language employing American teachers especially trained in this curriculum. Budgetary limitations did not permit the employment of more than 250 American teachers—a number totally inadequate to staff the schools. The teaching of English as a second language received its biggest boost in 1966 when Peace Corps volunteers were made available for this purpose. For the first time every school had an English-language teacher and major strides began to be made.

In the meantime, other questions were being asked by Micronesians and some Americans regarding educational objectives. A major study of education in Micronesia financed by Title III funds from the Elementary and Secondary Act of 1965 and conducted by the Stanford Research Institute resulted in the establishment of educational goals and a blueprint for action. At the same time, educational questions were being raised by local citizens, and a significant new force appeared. The Congress of Micronesia was established as the legislative branch of the government. This legislative body has full authority over most domestic issues and it has become apparent that they intend to exercise this authority over the educational program. The Congress passed legislation reasserting the control of district and local school boards and creating a new policy-making body—a territorial school board with both budgetary and policy-making power. One result has been to deemphasize academic and college preparatory curriculums and to establish vocational and technical education as a major component of the system. Because of these actions, the educational system in the Trust Territory during recent years has become rapidly Micronesianized, and far more authority is being placed in the hands of the community than is currently true in northern and western Alaska.

One cannot yet predict the long-range consequences of these events. However, several important trends are becoming evident for Micronesia and might well be considered for implementation in Alaska. These include the success of teaching English as a second language and the developing interest by Micronesians in the educational process. Research conclusively links the success of a child in an English-language school directly to his ability to use the English language competently. The English language capability–scholastic success ratio increases as the student proceeds to higher grades that demand greater English competence. Given this truism, it would seem only common sense to institute an intensive English-language program for all children who come to school speaking another language than English. In spite of this, teaching English as a second language in elementary schools is a very recent development in American education, and is still not well understood by many administrators.

Recent steps have been taken in Alaska to institute English-language courses in Indian and Eskimo schools. The trend should be encouraged and accelerated with special materials and teachers well trained in the language-teaching process. It should be emphasized that English-language competence serves a broad range of academic and vocational goals. It not only equips students proceeding on to college, but enables others to compete in industry. English is as much a vocational skill for the developing carpenter as his ability with saw and hammer.

Much greater attention must be focused upon English-language skills and the techniques of teaching them if we are to fulfill our responsibilities to the native child, whether in Alaska or Micronesia.

The Implication of Regional Folklore for the Health Professional

CORA S. BALMAT

MY INTEREST in anthropology and the implications of the methodology and thought system of this discipline for nursing began during my undergraduate studies at Louisiana State University between 1962 and 1964.[1] At that time we had instructors encouraging us to read Benjamin Paul, Ruth Benedict, Henry Lederer, and others, all names familiar to anthropologists, but fascinating and rewarding for this registered nurse coming back to school following thirteen years of experience in providing nursing services. I was formally introduced to anthropology in a course called cultural anthropology. I was asked to take the course to determine if it had relevance for nursing. At the time I was also enrolled in public health nursing and perhaps this is what led to my excitement over the implications of anthropology for the nurse practitioner. I began collecting data about folk medicine and folk remedies and although the implications of this knowledge for nursing practice seemed evident (Balmat 1964), I soon discovered they were not accepted by some members of the nursing school power structure.

In graduate school, my interest in anthropology continued. In 1966 I came to the University of Southern Mississippi, and theirs being a new school of nursing, tradition was not a problem. The faculty developed the philosophy and purposes and designed the curriculum. We had the temerity to state that the role of the nurse included participant observation, and we required a course in cultural anthropology (Report of Self-Evaluation 1969).

In the course of a curriculum project, I applied for a training grant for the integration of psychiatric and mental health concepts through the National Institute of Mental Health. The project required a cultural anthropologist as consultant. Because the University of Southern Mississippi had no anthropologist, we turned to Miles Richardson from Louisiana State University. Dr. Richardson developed guides for observing cultures and for obtaining responses to birth and death, as well as a description of how to recognize the patient as a person (Richardson n.d.a, n.d.b, n.d.c, n.d.d).

Examples of folklore encountered in Mississippi, Louisiana, and California during my nursing career will be used to illustrate the need for the health professional to understand the cultural characteristics of the society in which he practices. If the health professional is to help a community, he must learn to think like the community. Before attempting to introduce new health practices, it is wise first to ascertain existing health practices and to learn how these are linked to each other and the functions they perform. Some of the health practices I have encountered in nursing may at first sound weird. However, modern medicine is an extension of folk medicine and many useful remedies such as curare and opium and physical agents such as baths, massage, and surgery are derived from folk medicine. I have recipes from a book by a physician (Chase 1866) for treating various illnesses which are similar to potions being used in folk medicine. Yet today the medical world ignores or belittles current folk practices and beliefs.

My interest in folk medicine was aroused when I visited a newborn. He was asleep and everything about the physical environment appeared satisfactory. I observed two small straws lying across his anterior fontanel (in this culture called "the mole") and discovered that the purpose of the straws was to stop or prevent hiccups. The grandmother told me that if the mole is raised, the baby will have fewer colds than if the mole is down. As I continued examining this newborn, I noted an umbilical binder. The grandmother told me the band made the back stronger and the child would walk at a much younger age. Because stretching is considered harmful for the newborn, a piece of black cloth was tied around each wrist to prevent the baby from stretching.

Experiences like the following taught me tolerance for local customs. One adult patient was a diabetic, a double amputee, who had a hypertensive disorder. In assessing her in her home, I discovered her blood pressure was 240/140, her urine tested 4 for sugar, 4 for albumin, and positive for acetone. My first approach was to try to get her medical care; she informed me that she could not go to the clinic because her appointment card said that her appointment was due three weeks from that date. I called the clinic from her home and got permission to bring her for emergency care, but she adamantly insisted that her card said three weeks from today and that was that. What to do? I quickly recalled some of the biochemistry that I had struggled so valiantly to learn and began designing a program of home care. I determined from the patient that she took her insulin on an irregular basis, that she added much salt to her food, and in general would not follow the diabetic regime. I was honest and told her that her blood pressure was extremely high, that she had sugar, albumin, and acetone in her urine, and that her condition was serious. She looked at the test results and listened attentively to my suggestions. I outlined a program for her which included reduction of salt, increase in water, diabetic diet, and resumption of insulin injections. She agreed to this and then said, "I'll make a poultice of salt and vinegar and tie it on the back of my head." I questioned her about this practice. She said, "Well, I have to be awful careful not to put it on the top of my head as this will make the blood pressure go real high. But if I put it on the back of my head this will pull the blood down out of my head." My response was; "O.K. fine, you are going to make a poultice out of vinegar and salt and place it on the back of your head." I then restated the rest of the regime. When I returned the following week her blood pressure had dropped to 170/100 and her urine was negative for acetone, sugar, and albumin. She was convinced that what really took the blood pressure down was putting her salt and vinegar poultice on the back of her head. Certainly, the poultice was not harmful and the case illustrates that in assessing the coping abilities of individuals or groups, it is important to determine what strengths can be mobilized. Lack of awareness of cultural elements and unwillingness to incorporate folk medicine into the regime could have resulted in an alternate ending.

Ignorance of cultural determinants accounts for a failure. I once worked with a Mexican-American family in California where there were five children, each having a different father. The mother's current friend, father of the eleven-month-old child, lived in the home. There were numerous problems, and through use of community resources, many changes occurred. The couple sought counsel and got married, the husband attended adult school to learn English. But the mother received an unfavorable report from a Pap test and a biopsy was in order. She persisted in her refusal to have a biopsy. Several health workers as well as her family attempted to persuade her. Her response was fatalistic. There was a history of cancer in the family, and she would only consent to the biopsy if I could show her that this would be a 100 percent cure. A rate of 99.46 percent cure was found if early detection was accomplished. This would not do. Her stock answer was: "What will be, will be. If I have cancer, I'll die anyway. If I do not, it doesn't need to be done." Are there cultural determinants to explain her behavior?

I was able to reconcile folk remedies like the following with modern medical practice. For hepatitis, a large carrot is hollowed out and the patient urinates into it. The carrot is then hung on the patient's bed. When the urine has evaporated, the patient is allowed to get out of the bed and is cured. The treatment, my informant said, took from six to eight weeks. At that time, prolonged bed rest was an integral part of hospital therapy for hepatitis.

In the case of burns, the preferred folk treatment was to reburn the affected area. Is this a form of debridement?

A person with an elevated temperature is wrapped in leaves from the rice paper plant. These leaves are broad, with quite a heavy spine. An informant told me that the leaves are washed and dried and the heavy spine removed "so the patient will be comfortable." When my informant was hospitalized with "a fever in the breast," she was unable to get relief from treatment the doctor ordered. Her mother brought in some leaves of this plant and wrapped the patient's breast. My informant assured me her mother's treatment effected the cure. Fascinated by the story, and having applied many a compress, I placed some leaves from the plant on the dashboard of my car in the hot Louisiana sun for seven days. With temperatures in the nineties, the leaves failed to dry out enough so that they would crumble.

The logic of other folk practices eluded me, but I took note of them nonetheless. The treatment for mumps is most interesting. The person giving the treatment stands behind the patient and rubs the swollen gland with sardine oil, "rubbing up so that the mumps won't go down." Following this, the patient is fed the sardines and additional rubbing is done with an egg fried real hard, without seasoning.

Olive oil applied by a witch doctor was credited with curing a severe case of ringworm. Although the informant was also being seen by a skin specialist, she "knew" that the witch doctor's application had cured her.

"The strain," a local term for gonorrhea, is believed to be caused by menstruation. A new baby should not be handled by a menstruating woman because she will give gonorrhea to the child. Some protection is afforded the newborn if the woman wears a dime on a string around her neck.

"Soft bones" (rickets) are treated by combining "sweet oil" (olive oil), asafetida, and garlic, and rubbing this mixture on the baby for nine days. After the last application, the pan that contained the mixture is taken to the bayou and tossed over the right shoulder, downstream.

It would have been very easy to discount these beliefs and practices as superstitions and try to change the people toward more "scientific" courses of action. Knowledge acquired from anthropology made me explore the folkways, and knowledge of medical science seemed to indicate that what people were doing in their own way was, for the most part, not harmful. What harm are two straws crossed and placed on the baby's fontanel? What harm does a black string tied around the wrist do? For me, a member of another subculture in the South, to go into a home and attempt to discount these customs leads only to confusion, resentment, and hostility. However, it has been my experience that if I determine what the beliefs are and that they will not harm the individual, then it seems to work best to incorporate these beliefs and values and practices into the plan of care.

Desired changes in concepts of health can be accomplished when new methods are tied to old beliefs, practices, and values. This can occur if health workers become familiar with these cultural characteristics and when their education, training, and experiences sensitize them to people as they are in the community as it is. Change does not come easy, and it is natural to resist change that threatens basic security and is not understood. Changes in health care practices affect the total society. Haphazard changes result in disorder, even chaos. Before instituting change, it is essential to determine what additional modifications will be needed to maintain order in the total system. The nurse has an opportunity to gather data first hand, and, as Madeleine Leininger (1970) points out, nursing has valid contributions to make to anthropology. Anthropology's contribution to the health professional working in the South will be considerably enhanced when ethnographers publish more studies of the South (Pearsall 1966).

Although the health professional upon entering the community cannot begin a systematic ethnological study prior to taking action, he can utilize the observations made by ethnographers about his area. With this background as a base, he can proceed to observe the situation much as would the ethnographer.

The effective health worker views health from the focus of the people he or she serves. Failure to identify cultural characteristics has been responsible for some of the unsuccessful public health programs. Thus, identification of health beliefs will provide a more effective and comprehensive approach to medical problems as health workers become aware of the fact that they work in competition with folklore, ancient in origin.

NOTE

1.This paper was first presented at the 1972 annual meeting of the Southern Anthropological Society held in Columbia, Missouri, in the session on "Folk Concepts Relating to Physical Disorders."

REFERENCES

Balmat, Cora, 1964. Regional Folklore and its Implications for the Nursing Profession. (Unpublished paper.)

Chase, A. W., 1866. *Dr. Chase's Recipes* (Ann Arbor: published by the author.)

Leininger, Madeleine, 1970. *Nursing and Anthropology: Two Worlds to Blend* (New York: John Wiley and Sons).

Pearsall, Marion, 1966. Cultures of the American South. *Anthropological Quarterly* 39: 128–141.

Report of Self-Evaluation Prepared by the Faculty of the University of Southern Mississippi, School of Nursing, Hattiesburg, Mississippi. Based on the Criteria for the Appraisal of Baccalaureate and Higher Degree Programs in Nursing, 1969. (Unpublished paper.)

Richardson, Miles, n.d.a. Cultural Responses to Death: A Brief Sketch (Baton Rouge: Department of Geography and Anthropology, Louisiana State University). (Mimeographed.)

———, n.d.b. Cultural Responses to Health and Birth Crises (Baton Rouge: Department of Geography and Anthropology, Louisiana State University). (Mimeographed.)

———, n.d.c. Guide for Observing Cultures (Baton Rouge: Department of Geography and Anthropology, Louisiana State University). (Mimeographed.)

———, n.d.d. Who is the Patient and How to Recognize Him? (Baton Rouge: Department of Geography and Anthropology, Louisiana State University). (Mimeographed.)

The "Newly Applied" Anthropologist

CARL M. GUSSIN

THIS is a brief and very personal document detailing the problems encountered by one ethnographer, and to some extent by his family, when he moved from the academic enclave into the "majority culture" for the first time.[1] The problems raised herein are surely not unique, yet there is almost no literature dealing with them.

After five years in graduate school, one year of field research, and two years of teaching, I became directly involved with members of a majority culture of the United States when I was hired by the Institute for Behavioral Research to help implement a program aimed at preventing juvenile delinquency. In distinction to the subculture of the university, I came into contact with members of a culture characterized by a "commercial" worldview; a business must produce—that is, give the consumers what they want at a price they can afford—or go out of business. In the case of the "business" I entered when I left the university, production involved the following: a research task assignment, the completion and submission of monthly progress reports, evaluation of project progress, and new task prescriptions.

In the university subculture, achievement relates to a very personal worldview. To be promoted one publishes—and, possibly, teaches well. Many members within the academic subculture, however, do not want to be caught up in fiercely competitive achievement pressures requiring immediate, tangible production. Dr. Ronald S. Berman, recently appointed chairman of the National Endowment for the Humanities, described his transition from university professor to government administrator as without problem, and said that, in some ways, his new job—with its multidiciplinary nature—was more interesting than *just* teaching English. He said he liked the "hard edge of practicality" fundamental to his new position, and found it a refreshing change from the "famously misty" university arena. (Katzowitz 1972:12)

I think Dr. Berman's references to the "hard edge of practicality" and the "famously misty university arena" are critical to an understanding of the different cultures. Members of the university subculture are rarely under the gun, with assigned deadlines and weekly or monthly reports indicating what had been begun *and completed* the past month and what was planned for the coming one. And even more infrequently are the products of the academic community immediately analyzed, criticized, and turned back with the following marginal comments: "What does 'some (or many)' mean? Can't you count?" "Jargonistic bull!" "Don't use such wide generalizations."

The "mistiness" Dr. Berman referred to arises from the uncertainty in the academic world today. Many faculty, unsure of what students ought to or need to know, take refuge behind such platitudes as, "My students have learned to understand and to utilize their critical faculties." The "commercial" ethos with the requisite of immediate and tangible results, can hardly accept such generality.

Behavioral Programs in Learning Activities for Youth (BPLAY) is a preventive delinquency program composed of several discrete, after-school activities. Each of these activities is designed around an area of expertise of individual activity managers. Typical activities involve interior decorating, crocheting, film-making, photography, and social problem discussion groups. Ten program managers were budgeted for the first year of operation, January–December 1971.

The BPLAY program managers are hired by the implementing agency, the Institute for Behavioral Research, to work an average of six hours per week. Managers are recruited from the ranks of junior and senior high school teachers as well as nonteaching members of the community. The qualifications for the position of a BPLAY manager stress an interest in a skill of interest to the student population. The institute further develops the skills of these managers by providing them with additional procedures and methods of meeting their objectives in working with the students. Some in-service training is provided to the managers, as well as funds and work space for each of the programs.

The project's goal is to develop leisure-time activities to reduce antisocial behavior and prevent juvenile delinquency. The task of the ethnographer as delineated by the agency is to establish an initial base-line picture of the community and the students; identify student interests that could form the basis of the after-school program; find qualified resource personnel in the schools and the community to work as program directors for BPLAY activities; and to get a "sense" of the adolescent subculture and how it is perceived by the adults in the community.

The wide-ranging nature of the assigned tasks presented the first elements of culture shock faced by the newly applied anthropologist. Each of the assigned tasks could have comprised a whole, relatively large, research problem. The four together presented a seemingly overpowering set of tasks. This element of nonboundedness caused a major shift in the behavioral patterns of the ethnographer. Within the academic subculture there is a fairly well-defined set of behavioral patterns—preparing for and teaching classes at scheduled times, attending faculty meetings on a regular basis, and maintaining scheduled office hours and (generally scheduled) periods for research and writing. The routine becomes a known, familiar, and, therefore, easy pattern.

In the applied position, however, the behavioral parameters are almost unbounded. Since the ethnographer's tasks are so disparate, there is no chance to develop a routine—to "settle in." Because the research focuses on the adolescent subculture, the ethnographer's schedule is dictated by their behavior. At the same time, innumerable situations pop up with the community and the implementing agency, which require either a different utilization of time or a shift in research needs and methodologies. I, as ethnographer, have become, to some extent, a troubleshooter. In this kind of dynamic situation, strategies change from day to day under different situational stimuli and responses.

Another personal question is, "How does entry into a majority culture affect the lifestyle of the family of the (newly) applied anthropologist?" Probably the major adjustment lies in the use of time. At the university, I had a regular schedule, but my schedule as staff ethnographer is highly unpredictable. Sometimes I work for three weeks in the schools, researching from early in the morning till late in the evening. Other times, my mornings are spent writing and planning and, because of the nature of the project, I am in the community most afternoons and many evenings as well as weekends. I see much less of my family than I did while at the university. The adjustment has been slow and problem-laden.

One of the most unsettling aspects of working as an applied anthropologist is always having something more to do. Within the university subculture, I felt good after a particularly well-received lecture or upon completion of an article. The weekend ended a cycle, so I could relax. But the applied ethnographer rarely feels that a cycle has ended. There is always something else which should be done *now*. Time spent in nonresearch activity becomes tinged with guilt.

At the same time, there is always the nagging question, "Is my work satisfactory?" The ambiguity of the assigned task rarely allows clear feedback. A report is turned in, recommendations are made, and action may be taken immediately, soon, or not at all. In my case, suggestions are often implemented, yet questions of identity and worth arise. As a member of the faculty I felt that I had added to the totality; as an applied ethnographer, particularly a young one, I wonder if I have added enough. And what is enough? I knew better at the university.

A pervasive sense of isolation accompanies entrance into a "foreign" society. The subculture of the university, and, even more, the department, is relatively homogeneous. Differences are personal and idiosyncratic rather than normative and professional. Shared normative patterns, action symbols, and the idiom of the profession create bonds, even between conflicting factions. In the foreign society a greater degree of professional and personal heterogeneity emphasizes the differences in training, philosophies of life, and lifestyle between myself and other members of the project. Although I was hired as an ethnographer, neither the project director nor other members of the staff clearly understand what an anthropologist does or how he does it. Of course, this element of "not knowing" is a two-edged sword. That is, I, at times, am equally unclear about what the project director or implementor is doing, or why.

The first illustration of what I refer to as "not knowing" happened when I met a director of another institute project at a party. That director stated, "I don't understand why they (BPLAY) need an anthropologist; I don't know what you can do for them." For the remainder of the party I tried to explain to him—a member of the majority culture—what I, as an anthropologist, could add to the BPLAY project. Apparently he was impressed because he said that he had a problem on his project and he wondered if an ethnographer could help. Quickly, I sketched a few ethnographic activities I thought might be helpful to his project.

A second, more compelling example occurred soon after I accepted the position of staff ethnographer. A meeting was arranged with the designer of the program, the project director, the director of data collection, the institute statistician, and an operant psychologist on the BPLAY staff. The group originally expressed resistance to the potential of the ethnographer, so much so, that defining the parameters of the ethnographic task was held to be noncritical and, therefore, not to be included in the discussion of problems. But, as each problem was dealt with—data-oriented problems—it became clear that ethnographic input was basic to validity or reliability. What had begun as a meeting dealing with the nonethnographic components of the project became increasingly centered on the input of the ethnographer. The original problem of "not knowing" rapidly evaporated as the critical need for an applied ethnographer became apparent.

The third example of "not knowing" resulted indirectly from my research in one of the target schools. I had been working full time with the vice principal trying to analyze the patterning of disciplinary problems and disciplinary action. While studying this variable I became aware of the forthcoming move from the present condemned building to a new, modern building in the fall. Through participant-observation I noticed the low tension level concerning the physical environment of the old building; teachers and administrators did not penalize students for writing on walls or decorating hall lockers. I asked the vice principal what steps the administration had taken to try to insure a smooth transfer into the new building where a high premium would be put on maintenance. As a result of this intervention, the administration of the junior high school has planned a three-day teacher workshop in August to develop mechanisms for coping with problems related to the effect the new building will have on the behavior of teachers and students.

A problem of a very different nature arises from working in a majority culture establishment. I was invited to address faculty and graduate students at a university about my role as an applied ethnographer. I sketched the job and the problems as I saw them. One student asked accusingly, "Why invest so much money, so much time, and so many resources in that area? It's a middle-class community with middle-class problems. The need is in the inner city. Why aren't you there?" The question of need is an important question that applied anthropologists must deal with. Almost by definition, someone who chooses to apply his skills in nonacademic situations has made value judgments pertaining to need as well as relevance. This problem was thrown into sharp focus by the accusing manner of the questioner. Yet, how is need determined? Don't students in middle-class, white communities need, or is need something confined to ghetto areas?

Several concomitant considerations stem from the original question of need. The most pertinent one relates to the anthropologist's position when he is brought in to do a job but has no real decision-making powers—for example, power to influence the location of the project. A number of members of the academic subculture respond simplistically—"Don't take that job!" And yet, one of the basic tenets of applied anthropology requires the researcher to work within the limits set by an implementing agency rather than to reform that agency. Do we, as applied anthropologists, have the moral and professional right to remain uninvolved? In this situation the anthropologist straddles the fence—he is marginal to the academic community and only peripheral to the majority one.

The contemporary anthropologist needs guidelines established by behavioral scientists who work with complex social problems. The guidelines would, first of all, define objectives. Interdisciplinary cooperation among social scientists could produce a synergistic code.

This paper does not offer solutions or conclusions. I have asked questions and attempted to throw light on some of the problems confronting the anthropologist seeking to shift cultures. With the increase in professional anthropologists and the heightened competition for university positions, the problem of working outside the academic sphere is ever more critical. Applied anthropology asks, "How do we get members of the majority culture—BPLAY, the schools, the community—to know what we are capable of adding to their programs?" At the same time, the anthropologist interested in applied research, with ideas on how he can help, needs the refinement which can be acquired only from working within a majority culture for long periods of time.

NOTE

1. The research and experiences prompting this paper occurred during the first four months I was employed on the BPLAY Project conducted by the Institute for Behavioral Research, Inc., under the sponsorship of the National Institute for Mental Health, Center

for Studies of Crime and Delinquency, Grant MH—19706—01. I am grateful for the Institute's support and for the helpful comments of John Bis, BPLAY Project Coordinator, and Harold L. Cohen, BPLAY Project Director.

I wish also to express my appreciation to Marlene K. Gussin for her very considerable assistance in thinking through and writing this paper. An earlier version was presented at the 1972 annual meeting of the Society for Applied Anthropology, held in Montreal, Canada.

REFERENCE

Katzowitz, Lauren, 1972. Speaking for the Humanities. *Change* 4(3): 12.

Anthropological Perspectives on the Rehabilitation of Institutionalized Narcotic Addicts

C. Ronald Rosenstiel and Jeffrey B. Freeland

Anthropology, as a scholastic discipline, has not been traditionally connected with the practice of rehabilitative therapy.[1] With the increasing application of anthropology to contemporary social problems, however, such a connection has become not only inevitable but reasonable. Social scientists are becoming aware of the fact that it is short-sighted to consider the United States as a culturally homogeneous entity. During the formative stages of its history, the nation was pluralistic as a result of the ethnic variety of aborigines, immigrants, and slaves. More recently, pluralism increasingly reflects the incredible differentiation in our social structure attending urbanization. In short, subcultural differences exist in our nation, the extent of which we have yet to fathom.

Speaking dialects which are to some extent mutually intelligible and identifying ourselves as "Americans," we habitually ignore the fact that we know little of the way or meaning of life for countrymen occupying social strata other than our own. One little known subculture numbers among its participants a preponderance of narcotic addicts. This paper is addressed to two points: establishing the existence of a subculture surrounding the phenomenon of addiction, and presenting a conceptual model for the application of anthropology to the rehabilitation and resocialization of narcotic addicts.

Applied anthropologists can contribute to the rehabilitative effort on two levels. First, we can make treatment and rehabilitation professionals aware of the sociocultural aspects of narcotic addiction and the ways in which these carry their impact into the rehabilitative institution. Second, we can use social science perspectives to develop rehabilitative strategies especially tailored for members of the narcotic addict subculture.

There has been a trend, especially in the last decade, to conceive of criminality and drug addiction as social problems deriving from negative experiences within the family or society in general. Efforts at rehabilitation have moved concomitantly toward a medical model of therapy with particular focus on individual pathology.

Anthropology becomes relevant to the problem of rehabilitation when narcotic addiction is viewed not solely as a symptom of individual maladjustment, but as a phenomenon with characteristics of organization that allow it to be conceptualized in cultural terms. Anthropologists have only recently become involved in studying narcotic addiction, and our knowledge is still limited. As more is learned, however, features of cultural organization come to light which support our approach. Briefly, some of the salient aspects which point to the cultural perspective are: a dialect or argot which is highly specialized and only partially intelligible to nonaddicts; a social structure with a variety of well-differentiated roles which strongly regulates patterns of interpersonal relations both among addicts and between addicts and nonaddicts; a concept of social entity—addicts identify themselves as "junkies," like other junkies and different from "squares"; and differential association, in that addicts interact with squares primarily within exploitative or criminal frames of reference while their meaningful social life is carried on within a community of other addicts. These features, coupled with conventionalized daily behaviors centering around habitual crime and drug use, enclose a pattern of activities which are at least sufficient to comprise a meaningful lifestyle, albeit one that is strongly at variance with the values of the dominant society.

The allegation that narcotic addiction does serve as a focus for a meaningful style of life is persuasively argued by Preble and Casey. They write of narcotic addicts:

> Their behavior is anything but an escape from life. They are actively engaged in meaningful activities and relationships seven days a week. The brief moments of euphoria after each administration of a small amount of heroin constitute a small fraction of their daily lives. The rest of the time they are aggressively pursuing a career that is exacting, challenging, ad-

venturous and rewarding. They are always on the move and must be alert, flexible and resourceful. (1969:2)

Of course, the lifestyle is learned, and the learning takes place within a larger social milieu—typically an urban, lower-class situation. Sutter more precisely relates the addict to this setting:

> The term "righteous dope fiend" indicates a person who views the natural facts of life from a different angle. His behavior pattern and his set of background experiences in Urban America give him a unique style of life and a claim to fame. He rigorously uses the most expensive narcotics in the country. He is ranked by his colleagues as the most versatile of hustlers on the street scene, and "squares" refuse to tolerate his existence. (1966: 177)

In the same vein, Feldman documents how urban, lower-class ideology relates to addiction. Pointing to the pervasive values of personal autonomy, competence, and toughness which are personalized in the "stand-up cat," he notes that "drug experimentation can be seen as growing out of an ideological seed bed where rewards of high status and prestige are conferred upon action-seeking youth who strive to become stand-up cats by becoming involved in behavior that is exciting, daring, tough and dangerous" (1968:137).

Finally, it must be noted that not àll narcotic addicts participate fully in the addict subculture. Not all addicts derive from urban, lower-class backgrounds. In recent years narcotic drug use has diffused throughout the social structure. The core of the phenomenon, however, does remain in the inner city and it is the member of the addict subculture who poses the greatest challenge to rehabilitation.

The Narcotic Addict Rehabilitation Act (NARA) of 1966 established a new federal policy for the treatment of narcotic addicts. "The Act represents the view that narcotic addiction is symptomatic of an illness that should be treated and not a criminal circumstance itself" (National Institute of Mental Health 1968:2). The NIMH Clinical Research Center at Lexington, Kentucky, aside from fulfilling a research function, provides six-month in-patient rehabilitation programs for drug addicts, the overall purpose being to prepare addicts to live a productive life in an acceptable American tradition. We want to present an anthropologically oriented treatment strategy that would enable an addict who chooses to do so to become a more successful and acceptable participant in the major tradition of United States society. Secondarily, we are interested in pointing out some of the problems inherent in studying the culture of addicts. Our presentation draws upon data collected between October 1970 to January 1972 in the center, utilizing participant observation and open-ended interviews predominantly with black male addicts from urban areas.

Many addicts would like to make the cultural transition from the "fast life" (the cultural milieu of the street addict) to the "square life." First, several of the younger addicts we have talked to have tried the fast life and are ambivalent in regard to further participation in it. They would probably choose an alternative if it seemed to be realistically open to them. Second, there are stresses inherent in addict society that increasingly affect many addicts as they age. These stresses, when present, make leading the fast life more dangerous and difficult than usual. The addict's life is a demanding one, and as the individual ages, it is harder for him to keep up with the new tricks of young, energetic hustlers who are moving up from the bottom and trying to "knock him off" and "beat his game." In their words, it becomes increasingly difficult for an addict to "keep his thing together." Some addicts have been "busted" and incarcerated several times, and a third or fourth conviction would mean being "locked up for life." Third, there are those addicts who have been influenced by therapy and who would relinquish their former cultural ties if they believed that they could "make it with squares." For a variety of reasons then, there are addicts who are at least willing to try making the cultural transition from the fast life to the square world.

The addict who chooses to give up the fast life faces two problems. He must overcome his fear of entering the square world, and he must learn its standards for behavior. Since the fear of entry seems to be related to his felt inability to cope in the square world, we are faced with essentially one major problem, namely, teaching the addict an alien lifestyle and culture. To make the transition possible, it is hypothesized that the addict must become bicultural.

In order to know what an addict needs to learn or unlearn to become an acceptable member of the dominant society, we first must have a thorough knowledge of the culture he is leaving and the one he is preparing to enter. Knowledge of the square culture of the communities from which many addicts come is relatively accessible to researchers and clinicians, both through their personal experience and through a number of ethnographic works. In contrast, the culture of the addict, except in certain of its aspects, is only beginning to be known. Conceptualizing the culture of addicts is a major area in which anthropological expertise could be useful.

Several major problems, however, face the anthropologist studying a criminally deviant subculture in situ which make the use of participant observation as a data collection technique difficult (Weppner 1971). First there is the question of ethics. As a participant observer, the researcher would be witnessing and perhaps participating in illegal acts on a daily basis. Second, individuals who participate in illegal activities have a vested interest in keeping their involvement secret. Third, there is a great deal of danger in the situation. The social scientist could be killed or seriously injured by addicts for his money, or out of the fear that he might be a "narc" (narcotics agent) or a "snitch." He also faces the prospect of being "set up for a bust" by police and other officials as a result of his possible knowledge of "payoffs" to police or of other illegal activities. In addition, the researcher could be "busted" by honest officials for participating in or observing crimes. If arrested, the researcher could be placed in the unpleasant position of either divulging privileged information or facing a contempt of court charge. These reasons militate against the study of the culture of addicts in situ. The use of institutionalized addicts as a main source of cultural data offers a logical alternative.

The use of institutionalized criminals as informants also presents the anthropological researcher with problems. Many addicts have "done time" in state or federal penal institutions. These past experiences frequently influence an addict's initial perception of the Clinical Research Center. At least initially, the center is perceived as "just another joint" by many addicts, and they are suspicious of the clinical and research personnel. In addition, many of the addicts have committed crimes for which they have not had to "pay their dues." From their point of view, they are "in the joint" and anyone may be a "narc" or a "snitch." The researcher may be conceived of as attempting to uncover crimes committed by the informant or his friends. We believe these problems would arise when working with any institutionalized criminals.

In our research, we are dealing with the problem of obtaining valid data in the midst of distrust in several ways. Initially, we expend a great amount of energy conversing and interacting with addicts in informal situations and establishing trust bonds. We choose as research assistants addicts who are most trusted and respected by other addicts. (They are trusted because it is felt that they will not violate the ethic against "snitching.") The addict assistants are initially used as informants on the culture of addicts and later are used to collect information from other addicts. After acceptance by the addict population, it is possible to use participant observation in informal situations with more assurance that the data collected will be valid. Once the data on the culture of addicts is collected and analyzed, the development of a resocialization program for addicts who want to change their lifestyle is possible.

The anthropologist working to construct a resocialization program for addicts (or any other deviant group with culture) must begin by making a cultural comparison. If we compare cultural expectations of the two cultures, square and addict, we find three separate categories of knowledge: that of the addict, that shared by both the addict and the squares, and the square's knowledge.

These categories represent three learning fields to be dealt with in most situations. If we are comparing expectations in a social situation, at a party, for example, we find expectations specific to the culture of addicts. The first educational task is to make the addict aware of those expectations of the drug culture that would be inappropriate in square situations. Thus at a square party, an individual is not expected to bring drugs for others to share. There will also be expectations that drug addicts and squares share. The addict must be taught to differentiate these from the first type. Thus the addict, like the square, might be expected to bring a member of the opposite sex to a party and would be expected not to try to "make time" with other individuals' dates or spouses. In addition, we must differentiate those expectations attending a situation which are specific to the square culture. These must be taught as an additional cultural component to addicts. Thus an addict in his culture might be expected to stay at a party until dawn, whereas squares usually quit partying at two A.M. (the expectations particular to each culture are frequently in conflict).

The same comparative approach can be used in studying other cultural fields, including communication systems. For example, to communicate effectively and more rewardingly with squares, an addict must learn to differentiate between those items in his communication system which are not known to squares and those items the meaning and understanding of which he shares with squares; in addition, he must learn square words, gestures, and the meaningful use of space with which he is unfamiliar (see Edward Hall's [1968] studies of proxemics). Once the comparisons are completed in any cultural field, the problem becomes one of teaching the addict responses which would be appropriate in square situations.

In recent months, using the comparative approach outlined above, we at the Clinical Research Center have been developing an educational strategy aimed at promoting the addict's successful entry, through re-socialization, into the society of the major tradition. It will be instituted as an addition to one of the existing rehabilitation programs. The effort to date has been a collaborative one, involving research anthropologists, drug addicts, psychologists, psychiatrists, and social-work clinicians. The following briefly outlines some of the educational techniques we intend to employ in the near future.

Initially, we have chosen to reeducate addicts in areas most pertinent to their immediate success in some phase of square life. We will be working specifically with cultural patterns related to holding normal jobs, communication with squares, meaningful relations with people of the opposite sex, and obtaining pleasure in square society. Addicts often have trouble obtaining and maintaining normal jobs. They believe that they cannot communicate with squares, or understand "square broads" or "square dudes" (a problem many squares may share with them). They also find it difficult to anticipate much pleasure or excitement in living the square life.

Reeducation will involve lecture and discussion groups as well as practical resocializing experiences. Topics in the area in which the addict will be resocialized will first be presented in educational sessions. Briefly put, the culture of the major tradition will be explained and formally taught to the residents. Then, situations similar to those encountered in the square life will be reconstructed and presented to the addict in the institution. Addicts will be given many experiences in which they can test and use their newly acquired cultural expertise. At times, these situations will be monitored by closed circuit television and tape recorders, thus enabling the addicts and staff to critically analyze the addicts' progress.

During their last two months at the center, the residents will be given many opportunities to interact with squares, inside and outside the institu-tion, in a wide variety of social situations. As an example, an addict interested in a particular recreational activity or occupation will spend considerable time with squares who have similar interests. Addicts will also be given opportunities to participate in formal organizations and institutions in the community. Such activities include working in sports programs with youth, working in drug-abuse prevention programs, and counseling inner city youths. Participation in such activities should help create in the addict an awareness of and involvement in community activities.

Hopefully, experiences of this order will serve a multiple function. They will enable the addict to realize new interests while interacting with squares, thus breaking down his prejudice and fear of them. Also, outside contacts might prevent the addict from becoming overly dependent on the institution. Interaction with squares in real situations would also allow the addict and staff to evaluate the addict's newly acquired cultural expertise while he still resides in a therapeutic community. In addition, it would act as a testing ground for the rehabilitative personnel interested in improving and developing a resocialization program.

The rehabilitation of narcotic addicts involves, at least in part, their socialization into some phase of the major tradition of United States society. We see the therapeutic problem for those addicts who wish to change their cultural affiliation to be learning a new set of cultural standards. This resocialization approach has important implications for the organization of an institutional community. The ideal institution would be one which offered experiences that most closely approximated those to be met with by the addict in square life. The ideal institutional milieu would be one in which the staff's interactions with addicts most closely approximated their interactions with fellow squares. At some point in the rehabilitation program the role definition of the addict would shift from that of addict or ex-addict to one simply of person.

NOTE

1. This paper is a combined and briefer version of two separate papers presented by the authors at the 1972 annual meeting of the Southern Anthropological Society held in Columbia, Missouri, in the session on "Anthropology Politics: The Art of What Is Possible with Decision-Makers."

REFERENCES

Feldman, Harvey, 1968. Ideological Supports to Becoming and Remaining a Heroin Addict. *Journal of Health and Social Behavior* 9:131–139.

Hall, Edward T., 1968. Proxemics. *Current Anthropology* 9:83–108.

National Institute of Mental Health, 1968. *The Narcotic Addict Rehabilitation Act of 1966—A New National Policy.* Public Health Service Publication No. 1782 (Washington, D.C.).

Preble, Edward, and J. Casey, 1969. Taking Care of Business—The Heroin User's Life on the Street. *International Journal of the Addictions* 4(1):1–24.

Sutter, Alan, 1966. The World of the Righteous Dope Fiend. *Issues in Criminology* 2(2):177–222.

Weppner, Robert S., 1971. The Application of Anthropological Techniques to Understanding the Subculture of Addiction. Paper presented at the annual meeting of the Society for Applied Anthropology, April 14–18, 1971, Miami, Florida.

Action Research: The Applied Anthropologist in a Community Mental Health Program

STEPHEN L. SCHENSUL

THE OBJECTIVE of this paper is to describe the role of an applied anthropologist as it has developed over the last three years in a community mental health program in Chicago. The Community Mental Health Program was established in 1967 by members of the West Side Medical Center with funds from the National Institute of Mental Health. A segment of the lower west side, with black, Mexican and Middle-European populations, was chosen as the area to be served by the program.

The principle objective of the Community Mental Health Program is to provide free and highly accessible care to residents of the area. In-patient services at the Medical Center linked with "outpost" clinics located in each of the communities and staffed by full psychiatric teams are directed toward achieving this goal. A second priority of the Community Mental Health Program is participation in the process of community development—particularly in those efforts that are directed toward meeting the mental health needs of the area.

The Community Mental Health Program currently includes an anthropological component. It was the initial task of the anthropological research unit to provide information concerning the area's ethnic populations which could help in the planning and administration of the program and in providing more effective mental health services to residents. Our research unit was to collect information on the "natives" of the area so that plans, policies, and therapeutic methods could be developed to meet the special needs and cultural requirements of the black, Mexican, and Middle-European populations in our area. Our role was to aid the community *indirectly* by providing policy-makers and care-givers with the social and cultural information necessary to achieve the above objective. This position closely parallels the traditional role of the applied anthropologist—that of providing information to facilitate social-service programs established by the dominant policy-making and power sectors on behalf of economically and politically marginal groups in a society.

At the time the research unit was established, the Community Mental Health Program was at the end of its second year and was being deluged by pressing problems including conflict over community control and involvement, underutilization of services, and lack of indigenous personnel in the program. Our research data were to have helped solve some of these problems, but we soon came to feel that the clinicians, and to a lesser extent the administrative staff of the program, were neither open to new information nor flexible in their ideas concerning program development and provision of services. At the same time, the staff felt that the information we began to provide was not at all relevant to the problems they considered important. As a result, the inevitable communication difficulties arose between the clinicians and administrators and our research group. It became clear to us that information about the community and its various cultural and ethnic groups, no matter how good we believed it to be, was producing little interest and only minimal changes in the program.

However, unlike other research social scientists, the anthropologist has a built-in retreat mechanism which can allow him to move from a scene of institutional conflict to his natural zone of operations—that of the area under study. Thus we began to withdraw from intensive involvement in the clinical activities of the program. We turned to a search for new situations in which our research data could make useful contributions to positive social action. We found those action situations *directly* in the communities themselves.

Our research in these communities has concentrated primarily on the Mexican and Middle-European populations. These groups are clustered into a relatively narrow corridor—an east-west oriented segment clearly delineated from the rest of Chicago by physical and ethnic boundaries. The most striking characteristic of this corridor is the continuous movement of populations into, within, and out of the area. Mexicans, predominantly from Mexico but also from Texas, migrate primarily into the older section on the eastern end. Mexican-Americans who seek to improve their housing and economic conditions move into the relatively newer Middle-European section in the western portion of the corridor. Younger Middle-Europeans are moving out of the corridor to seek the suburban life west of Chicago.

Within the corridor, our research efforts have focused on the community in the easternmost section—El Barrio (a pseudonym). This area is particularly interesting because of recent and very rapid population changes that have taken place. This population transition was initiated in the late 1950s by the arrival of Mexican families who had been displaced by the construction of a highway and a university to the north as well as by the movement of many Middle-European families out of the area. The shift of population served to increase the flow of migrants from Mexico and Texas into the El Barrio community, with the result that the Mexican sector of the population has increased from 30 percent to almost 80 percent in the past decade. Most of the migrants in this period come directly from Mexico, specifically from cities such as Monterrey, San Luis Potosi, Guadalajara, and other urban areas in western and northern Mexico. Today, El Barrio is Chicago's port of entry and major residential enclave for Mexican immigrants.

The great majority of the new migrants have been born in Mexico. They speak Spanish and have only limited English-speaking capabilities. These people tend to maintain contact with Mexico, have a relatively low educational level, and have arrived in Chicago within the last ten years. Some individuals return to Mexico after accumulating financial resources, but the returnees are more than offset by an ever-increasing number of immigrants.

As a result, El Barrio has now taken on an overwhelming Mexican cultural orientation. Restaurants, taverns, groceries and supermarkets providing Mexican foods and services dominate the entrepreneural activity. This strong Mexican identity permits the non-English-speaking migrant to conduct essential activities in Spanish. Our information indicates that Chicago provides frequent job situations which do not require English language abilities; contacts through relatives and friends can lead to good jobs in Spanish-speaking work crews. An individual can operate quite well without speaking English, provided he limits his economic and social life to the El Barrio community. The lack of English facility nevertheless has its negative aspects for many. Migrants often remain uninformed and unarticulated as to opportunities and events both in the local community and in the wider society.

There is also an important, although smaller, segment of the community whose members have resided in Chicago for a long period of time, are bilingual, have a higher educational level, are skilled workers, and maintain a relatively high economic standard. These individuals show a bicultural orientation and remain in El Barrio because they choose to live in a Mexican community. These variations and other factors which indicate intra-ethnic diversity in El Barrio militate against any broad generalizations concerning the typical Mexican in the corridor area.

Our involvement in the El Barrio community began in traditional anthropological fashion, through participant observation and informal interviewing. We attended social, religious, and political gatherings, and frequented taverns, parks, restaurants, and night clubs—settings which permitted easy and informal interaction with community residents. Community leaders, social service agency personnel, clergy, and others well-informed on various aspects of life in the area were contacted and interviewed. However, throughout the first few months we felt as if we were operating on the periphery of community life. The Mental Health Program was a new institution initiated and directed by forces outside the community, and the concept of mental health was alien to El Barrio residents. Our applied research function in such a program was not particularly useful in establishing a clear-cut community identity.

As the first summer of research approached, a significant breakthrough occurred in our relationship with the El Barrio community. We learned that the staff of a settlement house in the area planned to spend the summer months in a program of community organization directed at a series of neighborhood groups or "block clubs" scattered throughout the neighborhood. Though the goals of the program were fairly diffuse, the general idea was both to make residents aware of problems in the community and to develop grassroots block organizations with which to deal with them.

From our initial impressions of community life, this seemed to us a highly significant program relevant to community needs and, at least in part, carried out by knowledgeable community people. It also seemed a way in which members of the research staff could develop contact with groups of community residents. Thus, without knowing exactly what kinds of contributions we could make, we offered our research services to the block organization program.

Since the block program was to begin almost immediately, we entered into a series of negotiations with personnel of the settlement house to establish areas of mutual benefit. It was decided that research personnel could be most helpful in participating in the organizing activities on the block and in making home visits to block residents. At the same time, researchers would be allowed to interview residents and carry out structured census and survey operations under the auspices of a community-based institution. The settlement-house staff also felt the anthropologists could make a special contribution by providing information to block team members and residents which would be useful in their block-organizing activities. Thus, researchers would participate in the action as well as conduct research to satisfy the informational needs of the settlement-house staff and the block residents.

Members of the anthropological research team were assigned to each of the block clubs. They were quickly drawn into activities such as organizing club meetings, obtaining signatures on petitions, developing street dances and fiestas, and collecting information on the attitudes of block residents toward such issues as garbage collection, street-cleaning, stop signs, urban renewal, and recreation facilities.

As research involvement in the block program continued, the settlement-house staff and the block residents became clearer about the kind of information they wanted from our research staff. The information they were interested in included minutes at block meetings and careful 'records of residents' participation concerning neighborhood and block issues.

As the summer progressed, our research staff became clearer about the kind of information we needed to promote the long-term goals of our research as well as the information that could be most useful to the administrative and clinical staff of the Community Mental Health Program. Interestingly enough, many of these needs could be well integrated with those specified by the settlement-house staff and neighborhood residents. In our research we carried out such procedures as detailed note-taking, collecting demographic data from a random sample of households, administering structured interviews, and analyzing kin and social relationships on the block. With these data we were able to supply relevant information to several different segments of the local community.

The block involvement had important implications for both the nature of our research and our relationship to the community. First, the elementary steps of organizing the block clubs provided significant entree for our fieldworkers and brought them excellent rapport. Fieldworkers were free to strike up informal relationships, to observe a wide sector of block activity, and to visit with large numbers of households on the blocks. Second, it showed an important sector of the action people in the El Barrio community that the resources and information we provided could make a significant contribution to the goals of their programs. Third, we decided to use the blocks (neighborhood segments of 100 to 150 households each) as the primary units for intensive ethnographic study throughout the corridor area. But the major gain of our participation in the block program was that it allowed us to conceptualize a research model which we have used consistently since then—that of "involvement in the action" as a major strategy in the development of an applied research project. The conceptualization of this strategy served to shift our focus from the Community Mental Health Program to the informational needs of action programs in the El Barrio community.

Three basic assumptions underlie the "involvement in the action" strategy: *Anthropological research should provide information to the population under study which contributes to the development of the community and the improvement of community life.* Such feedback of information should be direct, immediate, and localized. We are dissatisfied both with the kind of research that purports to contribute to some generalized pool of knowledge from which long-term benefits may accrue, and with the kind of research which suggests a pay-off to the population under study only after a long period of data-gathering and analysis. It has been our experience that research which has been sold to communities on these terms has rarely left residents feeling that they have profited from its results.

Programs for community development and improvement are most successful and effective when they are conceived and directed by knowledgeable community residents. While outside institutions and agencies can contribute special services to such development, it has been our experience that when the locus of power in community development programs is externally based, decisions which meet or satisfy community needs are rarely made.

Given the propositions stated above, we feel that *it should be the goal of our applied anthropological research unit to facilitate indigenous social action programs by supplying data and results which can make significant contributions to the effectiveness of their efforts.* We feel such a goal is best accomplished by the "involvement in the action" strategy as outlined in the steps below:

Step 1. Development of Rapport and Credibility of Applied Research. A great deal of the success of the "involvement" strategy necessitates a good working knowledge of the overall community and close relationships with important leaders and action people. It has been our experience that the depth of understanding and rapport needs to be far greater when one is seeking to make research results relevant to localized action, than when one simply desires access to an aspect of community life.

The knowledge gained from initial participant observation is most meaningful, and the continuing process of developing rapport is best accomplished when the field research is a full-time, year-round job; when there is a long-term commitment to the local area (we have found the development of step 1 demands the better part of two years); and when the researchers' residence, primary social network, and locus of activity are in the community under study. (In this point I strongly agree with Valentine [1968].) In these early stages of research, informational feedback plays an important part in identity building and demonstrates to community people that the information gathered can be of value to their action programs. In our work this feedback has included bibliographic surveys, reviews, demographic and census data, and results of initial structured interviews.

Step 2. The Identification of Significant, Indigenous, Action Programs. The applied researcher needs to identify the characteristics with which to establish the priority of action programs in the community. Such characteristics may include the program's relationship to community needs, the experience and competence of its personnel, its available resources, the reality of its goals, and the amount of support it has received from other community leaders and residents. However, unlike the traditional fieldworker, the researcher's own value system plays an important part in the kind of action he will seek to facilitate. Rather than avoid this issue, the researcher must balance the values and attitudes of the people in the community with his own ways of looking at the world before he commits himself to any program.

However, we have found that commitment to action programs in El Barrio depended less on carefully picking and choosing our involvement and more on events, pressures, and fortuitous situations in the community. Thus, while we began our involvement strategy with a calculated selection of action programs, we are now being recruited into a diverse and sometimes almost unmanageable number of efforts.

In traditional, university-based anthropology, the researcher shifts his operations to suit his own interests and that of his peers. There are also times when these shifts represent changing fashions in the discipline, pressures from university administration, and the changing interests of funding agencies. We learned very quickly that orienting research to the community meant that we were articulated to a different set of pressures—the actions, factions, successes, and failures that make up the reality of community life. Localized action has become the prime molder of our research operations and goals.

Step 3. The Negotiation of Cooperative and Reciprocal Relationships between the Applied Researchers and the Action People. The process of negotiation between researchers and community activists is most successful when the activists feel that the researchers can make a special contribution to the goals of their programs by fulfilling specific informational needs. Thus, while we are strongly advocating broad-based participation in community action, we feel that the researchers must base their usefulness on their ability to gather information that can contribute to program goals. At the same time, it is extremely important for the research group to make clear its motives in conducting the research. While motives and goals may change over the course of involvement in the action, most research groups usually begin with ideas concerning questions to be answered, populations to be sampled, and publication of materials. The more explicit these objectives are made in the initial negotiations, the easier it is to develop the rapport and trust needed for a good working relationship in the future.

The responsibility for identifying informational needs lies both with the action people and the research group. We have found that when resources are made available, community activists often request answers to highly sophisticated kinds of questions which involve complex interrelationships. Like modern anthropologists, they are not satisfied with low-level ethnographic descriptions. Such indigenously developed questions coupled with research ideas and perspectives derived from other field experiences and the literature can produce immediately useful data as well as raise important anthropological questions.

The negotiation of these cooperative and reciprocal relationships has direct impact on the activities of an applied research group. Successful negotiation, we have found, permitted us access to important aspects of community life, established our activities in a setting in which research operations could closely articulate to community action efforts, and exposed our operations to modification by new events and developments in the community.

Step 4. Initial Participation in Specific Action Programs. This step may be seen as similar to 1, except that the researchers focus their observations on specific action programs and the populations they will effect. In this step, the emphasis is on helping to establish the particular program, which frequently requires the researchers to participate in activities which may have little to do with data collection. It is a period in which rapport development and assessment of the program are the primary goals. An additional benefit in these early stages is the ability to document the development of the action program itself. Such information is essential to assess its eventual impact on residents and in understanding the organizational life of the community.

Step 5. The Identification of Specific Informational Needs of the Action People. In the initial stages it is hard to establish what kind of information the people in a specific program require, or in turn what the researchers can provide. As the action becomes more defined and researchers become more involved, specific, almost contractual arrangements can be worked out for supplying information that closely articulates with the goals of the program. In establishing these kinds of contractual arrangements between the researchers and the action people, we have found that research results have a higher probability of being useful when people in the community who are involved in programs play an important role in the development of research concepts and strategies, and when community and program people help in the collection and analysis of data.

Step 6. Meeting the Needs of Long-Range Research Plans. Although our focus in this paper has been on the relationship of research to community action, our applied anthropological group maintains a set of research goals which have developed out of more theoretical psychological and anthropological issues. This aspect of research has not developed out of community-action situations, but we feel these data will have relevance to such action in the future. One great strain for our research unit is the need to adhere to our long-term research design and, at the same time, satisfy the short-run informational needs that result from our "involvement in the action" strategy.

Our long-run intention is to examine the sociocultural concomitants of mental illness among the Mexican and Middle-European populations of our area. Sometimes the data required for this goal can be collected in the process of conducting the more immediate applied research. For example, in a project to assess the attitudes of parents concerning a school in the neighborhood, we were able to include many questions which gave us important household and family data. Similarly, in a project to assess block residents' attitudes and involvement with block clubs, we were able to collect important census and demographic data and to select samples for more extensive sociocultural and psychological interviewing. Thus, research operations that were designed to meet short-run informational needs have served as pilot materials and pretests for the hypotheses and concepts in our long-term research design. These procedures are much like those described by Glazer and Straus (1967) in the development of "grounded theory."

There are times, however, when such compromises do not work out and it becomes necessary to separate long-term and short-term research operations. We have frequently found that some of the research conceived of as part of a long-term design have provided data which could be fed into community-action situations much more rapidly than we expected. Such long-term and more academically oriented operations must be clearly stated to action and program people and carried out with their approval and understanding.

Step 7. Formalized Research and Data Collection Operations. Throughout the initial period of involvement in the action, informal interviewing and participant observation techniques are used and minutes of meetings and other general fieldnotes are recorded. In the later stages of the action when more rapport has been developed and operations can be more clearly worked out, techniques such as structured interviews, census operations, and attitude and value interview schedules can be administered with relative ease. This is particularly the case when the structured operations are designed in collaboration with action people and administered by community residents.

Step 8. Analysis of Data. In any action situation there is a great deal of pressure to produce data as fast as possible and at a time when it can be of maximum benefit to the planning and execution of an action program. Unlike more academically based research, the time within which research results are produced is vitally related to their usefulness. The "involvement in the action" strategy requires the development of procedures for the rapid analysis of data utilizing simple and easily manipulated techniques. At the same time, more sophisticated techniques are used to serve less pressing action needs as well as the long-term research goals.

Step 9. Data Dissemination, Evaluation, and Interpretation. It is frequently assumed by the researcher that simply making information available to individuals will have a powerful effect on their planning and actions. In fact, we have found that if information is to have an impact it must be continually reformulated and reinterpreted to suit the changing situations and needs of recipients. The applied researcher must be involved not only in presenting but also in mediating, negotiating, and interpreting the results so that they may make a contribution to specific situations.

We have found that distributing written material is usually not the best way to disseminate research results. Seminars, lectures, consultations, and participation in planning sessions have usually proved to be more effective.

Utilizing a variety of data-distribution techniques tends to increase the impact of research findings on action. One example involved data gathered from the families of parochial school students. Information which we had collected on parents' attitudes, aspirations, and background was presented to parents at a P.T.A. meeting at the school. We used handouts, illustrations, slides, and an oral presentation in both Spanish and English. Parents reacted quite positively, and for us it was one of the most satisfying sessions we have had in the community.

We have found that when data dissemination has been coupled with an "involvement in the action" strategy, the researchers are frequently asked to participate in the planning of subsequent courses of action and in decision-making. Such participation serves to increase the researchers' commitment to the action as well as their responsibility for any successes or failures that may result.

Disseminating data to community groups allows criticism, evaluation, and assessment of the results to be rapidly fed back to the researcher. In academically based research, heavy publication backlogs mean long delays in exposing results to the public and colleagues. Frequently, critical reactions to published papers or even those read at discipline meetings are nebulous or nonexistent. In the "involvement in the action" strategy, results are immediately exposed to scrutiny by knowledgeable community people and subjected to tests of validity by subsequent events and actions. Such a powerful feedback process plays a much stronger role in the production of quality research than does the feedback from groups relatively unfamiliar with the research situation.

We are currently utilizing the "involvement in the action" strategy in three different action settings in the El Barrio community. One of these programs serves Chicano addicts in the community. Run by a group of Chicano ex-addicts who are bilingual and bicultural, its intention is to meet the needs of the addict by utilizing the Chicano community experience. The program operates on the assumption that the individual was a Chicano before becoming an addict and that his success in defeating his habit is tied to his return to his culture and community. In this program the applied research group is helping with discussion groups, engaging in general participant observation, developing interview schedules for assessing the background and addiction situations of members of the program, and conducting individual interview sessions. Data collected from these activities played an important part in developing a proposal that was recently submitted to the National Institute of Mental Health to fund what is currently a volunteer-run program. (We have recently received word that this program has been funded for an eight-year period.)

A second program seeks to establish a community-based, community-controlled training program for Chicano mental health workers in the El Barrio area. Its objectives are: to increase the number of Chicano mental health practitioners, to develop more effective and culturally relevant services for Chicano populations, to create new therapeutic models appropriate for Chicanos, and to create a change in mental health facilities so that these institutions can become positive resources to the El Barrio community. Our applied research group helped form a committee to deal with mental health problems in the community, supplied data concerning the structure of mental health institutions and mental health resources in the community, and documented community mental health needs. Once again our research data played an important part in developing a proposal which recently received funds from the National Institute of Mental Health.

A third program established a multipurpose community center in El Barrio. The center, serving both youths and adults in the community, has developed programs in education, health, mental health and vocational counseling, Chicano cultural arts and history, recreation, and community development. This program utilizes the skills and resources of a large and active group of community volunteers in combination with specialized services provided by personnel and organizations in the El Barrio community. As a community-run, community-financed center it not only provides a new and effective facility but is also a resource which can help to make all service programs more relevant to the needs of residents. In working to establish this center, our applied research group has contributed a very broad range of data drawn from a number of community settings, and members of our group have also participated in planning and decision-making. The community center promises to be the central facility in the El Barrio community, and we are currently planning a whole range of research operations to facilitate its diverse programs.

It must be emphasized that our "involvement in the action" strategy in articulating research to community action is being carried out from the base of the Community Mental Health Program. Our work has received the financial and moral support of the administrators of this program, who see our activities both as providing basic research data to the program, as well as contributing to the community-development aspect of the Community Mental Health Program. We feel it is to the credit of the administration of the Community Mental Health Program that we have been allowed to pursue, with a great deal of freedom, our direct role as information-providers within the communities.

As our research has taken on a stronger community base, our relationships with the clinical staff of the Community Mental Health Program have improved considerably. Much of the information we had initially presented had been irrelevant to their clinical activities. We were presenting community-level information which they found difficult to translate into their individual counseling activities. We found much greater success when both the anthropological and clinical staff sought, in discussion, answers to common questions with each anxious to benefit from the other's perspective. This exchange of information has had the following advantages: Both groups recognize and respect each other's experience and fund of information; a common area of interest is established; each group shares an equivalent responsibility to come up with solutions from its own unique perspectives. This process of negotiating and interpreting data so that it fits the specific needs of recipients comes directly from lessons we have learned in the community as a part of our involvement strategy.

We have, by no means, solved all the problems of communication within the Community Mental Health Program. Interaction with psychiatrists, psychologists, social workers, administrators, and other members of a complex bureaucracy present another whole range of factors that have played a significant role in the development of our research activities. These relationships obviously require a detailed discussion in and of themselves. However, the lesson here is that professional groups and service institutions have their own culture, values, attitudes, and behaviors of which the anthropologist must be as well aware as he is of the community and its residents.

The "involvement in the action" strategy seeks to facilitate indigenous social action and community development. It establishes an approach to anthropology that makes the community both the object of study and the most important recipient of the results of that study. The power and leverage that come from these data are thus in the hands of community residents rather than being controlled, no matter how benevolently, by external institutions and power structures or by the professional status-seeking activities of the anthropologist. The key to the development of this strategy is the articulation of our applied research group to people, programs, actions, and events in the El Barrio community. These forces shaped the goals and strategies of our group so that our research has now become a community facility serving community needs. At the same time, the action-oriented research has contributed valuable data and perspectives which we believe will significantly enrich our long-term research results.

REFERENCES

Glazer, B. G., and A. J. Straus, 1967. *Strategies for Qualitative Research* (Chicago: Aldine).

Valentine, C., 1968. *Culture and Poverty—and Critique and Counter Proposals* (Chicago: University of Chicago Press).

Problems in Government Anthropology

JAMES W. HAMILTON

SOME GOVERNMENT officials have come to realize that directing technical development in an underdeveloped area is not a simple process.[1] I was recruited for a United States Agency for International Development (USAID) project in Tanzania because an official there came to the conclusion that many technical assistance projects fail not for technological but rather sociological reasons. He insisted, over the objections of Washington, that a social scientist be included on the project team, but he was unclear as to how to use one in the field; he was not sure what contribution the anthropologist could make; he did not understand how the anthropologist goes about his work of collecting and analyzing data.

I had long wanted to be involved in a program of directed culture change in order to test some of my ideas about how change happens and how one could go about making it happen in constructive and least disruptive ways. Hence I welcomed the good fortune to be asked to apply my training and general knowledge to a problem of directed agricultural and social change in East Africa with which, however, I had no previous experience. Unfortunately the results were not very successful in securing the expected changes.

This paper is concerned with what went wrong. I believe the situation in directed culture change is generally such that failure is built in, and I suspect that success in applied anthropology is often accidental. However, I am not willing at this point to generalize to all of applied anthropology. Clearly there have been some successes. The present discussion will therefore be somewhat personal in that the difficulties are those I encountered while working on two projects in Tanzania involving the United States Department of Agriculture (USDA), the Near East Foundation, USAID, and the Ministry of Agriculture of the government of Tanzania.

My first field research had been carried out during a two-year period among the tribal Karen of Thailand with an additional six months' redy ten years later. There was no government connection of any kind. My government-connected research in Tanzania was carried out among the Kuria and the Masai, with a one-year gap between projects, for a total of one and one-half years in the field. In both the government and nongovernment situations the research problem was similar; it concerned culture contact and change in a tribal group within a developing nation. A major difference was the fact that in the government-connected research, the change was planned and directed. This crucial difference led to quite different kinds of research strategies.

I was recruited for the first project in Tanzania through a very haphazard procedure. I had no experience in applied projects, and I had never worked in Africa. Yet a USDA official walked into my office one day and asked if I would like to go to Africa on the off-hand suggestion of my name from a colleague of mine in rural sociology. It happened that I had been seriously considering doing some research in Africa to broaden my anthropological perspective and research background and had already applied for a leave of absence from the university to do a restudy in Thailand. I therefore jumped at the chance to go to Africa and planned to carry out my restudy in Thailand as well. However, the fortuitous circumstances under which I was hired worried me.

When I was first recruited by the USDA official, I asked the name of the group to be affected by the project. He did not know, and did not know that it was important to the project. When I arrived in Washington, D.C., to be briefed on the project by USAID officials (USDA recruited and then "loaned" personnel to USAID), I asked again. They did not know either. In fact, nothing was known of either the language or culture of the people in the project area. Only the location of the project on a map was known. (The briefing was superficial and dealt mainly with bureaucratic, administrative matters.) Judging from the map, the people could have been either Luo or Kuria, who are quite different and speak unrelated languages. I discovered they were the BaKuria only after I arrived in East Africa. How much time I could have saved, how much information I could have collected had I known this before leaving the United States!

The project among the BaKuria was a feasibility study to determine, outline, and develop a budget and scheme involving consolidation of fragmented land holdings, improving crop production, as well as introducing some new crops. All of this implied changes in the social and economic organization of the society (Hamiliton 1969). The team of specialists, under pressure to come up with a working plan with which to start the project, devised one which was premature and had several unresolved problems, such as how to deal with households having plural wives, and how to deal with the cattle population. The plan, however, was never implemented, but had it been, this team would not have done it, thus breaking the continuity of planning. I considered the reasons for its non-implementation to be an important part of my research, but they were not viewed as such by USAID.

The second project, among the cattle-herding Masai, was the other side of the coin in that it involved implementing a feasibility study in the development of which I had no direct part. However, many of the general orientation statements I had made concerning culture change in the Kuria study were incorporated in the final USAID Masai proposal for funding. This plan, too, had some serious flaws, such as the failure to take into consideration the relation of cultivators and herders to each other and to the land, or the settling of grazing, occupancy, and water rights. The project appears to be failing due to planning flaws and to ideological differences between USAID and the Tanzanian government over project goals.[2] The legitimacy of the project has been seriously questioned by the Tanzanian parliament.

I would like now to present briefly the strategy that emerged from my two experiences in programs of directed change. Clearly, the role of the anthropologist when he applies his method and theory to reality to effect change is very different from his role in traditional ethnographic research. The anthropologist must carry out research on the cultural group to be changed, but he also must include, as an integral part of his research, data on the change agents (see also Foster 1962:249). This does not imply two separate research projects, one on the target culture and one on the bureaucracy (which are later articulated somehow), but rather a single, integrated project that involves both. The unit of analysis in research and its application in directed culture change is a sociocultural network that may include individuals from different cultural traditions and with different goals and values. I believe this makes applied research more difficult. In my situation, the unit of analysis included two governments as well as the tribal cultures. Along with appropriate formal techniques, the role of the anthropologist must involve participant-observation in order to develop rapport with and understanding of the tribal culture on the one hand, and government officials on the other. His role is that of a cultural middleman, as well as an advisor to members of the technical team. In other words, research is carried out along a continuum from the high levels of government policy-making and planning agents to the on-the-ground, day-to-day activities of tribal members. In between are found the actual technical innovators. The anthropologist must not only carry out research along this continuum but must also make suggestions for changes in behavior along it, and he must attempt to get individuals all along it involved in planning, innovation, and evaluation (Kuria and Masai were often left out of project planning). I do not mean to imply that the anthropologist stands outside this process and somehow directs or manipulates it; he must be involved in it. This is why participant-observation is important and necessary. However, the role does involve a stance of neutrality. The anthropologist cannot be viewed as "for" or "against" anything—except "for" helping both sides; otherwise he will be unable to collect unbiased data. He, therefore, cannot be directly involved in specific acts of innovation. However, the anthropologist can and should operate as a catalyst, introducing new ideas for individuals in the continuum to talk and think about, then adopt or reject; their reasons for doing so are also the province of the anthropologist. He may then analyze and reevaluate the data which should result in new directions for attempted change. The innovative aspects of the anthropologist's role will involve (1) his identification of problems of development—all along the continuum, (2) discussion of these with individuals involved, (3) suggestions for specific changes or approaches, both technical and social, that will implement or change government policy and "test" the tribal culture for points of "easy" change, and (4) providing information which may be used for program development, change, and evaluation.

There is, however, a danger in this strategy; if the anthropologist is carrying out research on the innovators as well as those to be changed, he may be viewed as a threat and may be seen as disloyal to the bureaucracy or the project or the tribal people or all three.

There are, then serious handicaps that must be overcome by the anthropologist who wants to take his talents beyond the university. These are of two sorts: those arising from structural characteristics of the recruiting and supporting agency, involving information, policy, planning, and organization; and second, those arising from the traditional research strategy used by the anthropologist which views research on merely the target culture as all that is relevant to problems of change.

I have no reason to assume that my situation or the projects discussed here are unique. On the contrary, I have good reason to believe the issues are more general and are relevant to the future of anthropological research and application. One has merely to read the literature to see that others have encountered similar difficulties. Barnett (1956:49) says, "No matter how tactfully it is phrased, the truth is that anthropologists and administrators do not, on the whole, get along well together." Foster (1962:241) says, "The history of anthropological participation in developmental programs is pretty much one of frustration, misunderstanding, and lack of good communication between administrators and scientists." I contend that the issue is not a conflict of personalities but rather a structural and a conceptual one.

I wish to emphasize that the experiences discussed in this paper have not yet led me to reject the idea that anthropologists should sometimes be involved in government-connected research on development programs. Probably more anthropological endeavor will be called upon to solve specific social problems (see Goodenough 1962). Undoubtedly, we will not be completely free to do anything we want on any project that we choose. In addition, our research subjects will more often use the option to reject our attempts to do research among them. The need to worry now about the limitations and requirements we are willing to accept before they become rigid has been a stimulus for this paper.

Several critical issues are involved in the bureaucratic process of recruiting anthropologists for specific government projects. One is that the government, or the private agency contracted to recruit for the government, apparently lacks a store of information on specialists and their availability for projects. At least, information that is available (such as the national roster of professional skills maintained by the National Academy of Sciences) apparently is not used.

If government agencies are seriously going to use the talents and perspective of anthropologists, they should systematically recruit the best available people. Otherwise, a great deal of time may be wasted while the anthropologist gains the necessary background, and it is less likely that the project can be successful or benefit from the use of the anthropologist if he is not trained for the area where the project is located.

Another issue arises because government agencies do not know what information they ought initially to have in hand to give the anthropologist. If the government is serious about our potential contribution to development projects, it should seek to become aware of what information is important, both for its own personnel and for the field anthropologist. Would it not be logical and more efficient to employ an anthropologist as full-time consultant to agencies involved in projects for non-Western cultures? He could collect relevant previous research data and make initial briefings useful to all field technicians. As one author puts it, "where in Washington . . . are the staffs whose function is to sift and appraise the conclusions of relevant research for administrators. . . . Where, with periodicals as numerous as insects, is there one devoted to the critical consideration of the consequences of specific research" (Orlans 1968: 158). And, I might add, where is there in government an agency or individual responsible for gathering information on specialists available for development projects, and where is the agency that gathers pertinent background information on project areas with which to brief the specialists?

It is true, of course, that much anthropological research is not directly relevant to development projects, and it is no doubt the case that anthropologists do not appreciate the problems of government in attempting to implement a project in a foreign country where there are economic and political implications beyond the scope of the particular project. Nevertheless, anthropology has a unique contribution to make toward all of these problems if our claims are true.

Once a development project has been roughed out and the personnel chosen, there are still problems of structure, organization, and timing the project implementation. Such issues arise as the matter of implementing a predetermined policy and plan versus undertaking research to develop feasible goals consistent with both the cultural situation and government policy and then implementing a dynamic plan that may be altered as the project proceeds. A critical issue is the point at which the anthropologist enters the scene. Is he to be allowed to enter the field early, before other technicians arrive, to gather background cultural information to be used in developing the plan and to feed information to other technicians? In both projects in which I was involved, all personnel began working at nearly the same time. I, therefore, had no time to collect basic data useful to the project before the technicians began attempting changes or making recommendations. There was also little appreciation of the time an anthropologist needs to understand the situation in which he works. Officials generally acted as if they believed that cultures only operate from nine to five and that project personnel must be "busy" during that time. When I insisted on learning some Swahili, the other project technicians reacted first with surprise and then complained that I was wasting time. It was difficult to convince AID that some of my research data had to be collected on American and Tanzanian bureaucratic characteristics, which meant that I could not be "in the field" all the time. It was not understood that I had to carry out research apart from other technicians in order to develop the more than superficial rapport necessary to collect detailed sociocultural data. Often "windshield surveys" carried out by the whole team were considered research. They expected me to hop out of the car from time to time and ask some native person a question or two. Some of my own research was seen as merely "having a good time" by "socializing with the natives."

The position of the anthropologist in the organizational framework should be as unambiguous as possible. His specific duties and contributions, by their very nature, are already ambiguous and miscomprehended. In the Masai project, I was hired by the private Near East Foundation (under contract to USAID); I was under the direction of local USAID officials who viewed the technicians as a team under an American team leader, but I was also an employee of the Tanzanian government, which viewed us as individual civil servants responsible to its rules. It was not clear to anyone what I was expected to contribute to the project. Indeed, I was considered excess baggage by some.[3] Both the Tanzanian and American governments saw me as a salesman or miracle worker in transforming Masai social customs, and they were disappointed when I could not produce immediately. USAID was ambivalent concerning my desire to do additional research in a control area, where no project work was being carried on. The Tanzanian officials believed such research unnecessary since they "already knew all about the Masai." The two governments could never agree on either the primary goal of the project or my role in achieving it.

All of this raises the issue of the specific role of the anthropologist. It seems to me that the training and perspective of the anthropologist makes him uniquely qualified to play the role of cultural middleman between high-level planners and policy-makers on the one hand, and the people to be affected by development schemes on the other hand. This clearly implies that an anthropologist should be involved from the very beginning, and that one should stay involved through the stages of implementation. It is not necessary that it be the same anthropologist in both cases, although that would provide better continuity. The anthropologist needs a great deal of information on the general policy orientation of planners as well as information on the cultural system to be affected. Once the general plan and organization is settled, the anthropologist must carry out independent research on the tribal group before implementation is begun so that he may make suggestions and predictions as to what will and will not work in the process of introducing new ideas, techniques, and social relations within the general policy context of the project. Of course, it would be extremely helpful if some information were in hand even before the general policy for an area is firmly established. And research must continue throughout the project since conclusions will change as the situation changes, an idea which is particularly difficult to get across.

In the first project, the United States planners believed that I could gather relevant information for the project in at most two or three months. I had to argue with them in order to be allowed to carry out research for six months and was successful only because the local USAID official supported me. In the second project I was expected to be merely a kind of supersalesman and troubleshooter: I was to convince the Masai to do what was required by the planners. My demands that I be permitted to do social research on Masai culture were finally tolerated but not supported or understood. I carried out one year of research on Masai culture, but since my research needs were not actively supported, it was inefficient, and the innovative suggestions that I made were often ignored.

I am not suggesting that the anthropologist is always right, or that everything he says should become policy or be implemented. However, if the anthropologist is to be useful in a project involving social change, then he should be included early in the planning and organization; he should be concerned with project design and implementation procedures; he should start his work before other technicians and have enough lead-time so that he has hard information to feed to them as they begin innovations of a technical nature; and, he should carry out ongoing research and be involved in a continuous evaluation of progress.

These kinds of misunderstanding can be overcome by the anthropologist if he is willing to take the time and patience to explain what he is about and how he must operate. He must take time to explain why his work is different from that of other technicians and what contributions he believes he can make. He must, finally, show some positive results from his participation in the project. On the Kuria project, I arranged to have several sessions with all the technicians to talk about various aspects of planning and for each of us to discuss our potential contribution and methods of work. These discussions contributed to the development of a working relationship among the project technicians and USAID officials. They were successful enough that I was invited back a year later to participate in the Masai project. On the Masai project, the same procedure was instituted, but since it was an implementation project and more complex than the Kuria project, there were some differences. African officials were involved in the discussion sessions that were held once a month. Problems of implementation were discussed, points of difficulty were brought out, seminars were given by the various technicians, the officials presented their positions, and monthly work plans were arranged.

Assuming that the structural and role problems can be solved, there are still important considerations concerning anthropological application in project implementation. For example, what general theoretical stance and methodological orientation appears to be most useful in this kind of situation? George Foster has stated part of the answer very well and I will quote him:

> [The anthropologist's] most important contribution to action programs is an unusually broad and flexible field research methodology, based on a holistic view of society and culture and using general concepts such as cultural integration, cultural dynamics, sociocultural systems in contact, and the premises underlying cultural forms as a means to structure research and interpret results. Anthropological field research is exploratory and wide ranging, and in contrast to the more elaborate research methods

of other social sciences, it is relatively unstructured. But in directed culture change programs, where the technical, social, cultural, economic, psychological, and other pertinent factors are almost infinite and usually not recognized in advance, this exploratory quality is enormously advantageous. It vastly increases the investigator's chances of hitting upon critical elements in any specific situation, simply because the anthropologist is trained to examine the entire spectrum of the culture he studies. (1969:57–58)

One could argue with some aspects of the approach expressed by Foster. Indeed, I found that it left project administrators unimpressed. They wanted specific answers to hard questions of implementation. It is true, of course, that Foster is talking about information-gathering, but if the information cannot be translated into action, then the anthropologist will find himself ignored. Goodenough, in fact, chides us rather harshly for our qualitative approach when he says,

The essentially journalistic approach to ethnography . . . falls short of supplying the kind of ethnographic intelligence that is often needed in action situations. So, also, does the approach to ethnography exemplified by some members of the sociological school of anthropologists, who describe what they observe in terms of a general theoretical system of a logico-deductive sort using the community under study to exemplify their ability to apply the concepts of their *a priori* frame, and to demonstrate that . . . it is possible to find a way of interpreting it so as to make it appear that in some respects it contributes to the continuity of the community. (1962:175–176)

Goodenough's answer is to develop "a 'dictionary' and 'grammar' of social conduct" (1962:176). I will not argue the merits and demerits of Goodenough here, but it does seem to me that his attitude misses the point that the anthropologist often cannot do "normal" research in government-connected programs, and much of the results of normal research would probably not be useful for the specific program. Since the research situation is different in programs of directed change, the anthropologist must alter his strategy.

I agree with Goodenough (1962:173), and with Pelto (1970:49), on the need to operationalize concepts. It also seems to me that the general, qualitative approach advocated by Foster, although allowing more flexibility in the research setting, is incomplete. The approach adopted must take into account more than merely the target culture. The job of the anthropologist in change programs is two-fold. He must gather relevant information and he must see that that information is applied in directed social change. As I indicated above, the role of the anthropologist must be that of a cultural middleman or impartial intermediary (Barnett 1956: 88). This implies that the research setting includes not only the target culture but the innovating one—or aspects of it—and the technicians as well (see Foster 1969:90ff.).

This paper is the result of my frustration, lack of experience, and attempt to develop a research strategy appropriate for a situation of directed culture change in which no one controls all the relevant, causative factors, and in which some general goals may be contradictory. I spent a great deal of time in discussions with both African and AID officials, as well as with the technicians on the project. I spent a great deal of time, as well, studying both Kuria and Masai culture. Much of the material presented here was verbalized to both sets of government officials and it helped us all to see the difficulties. Subsequently, both governments acted in terms of my analysis (Hamilton 1971). The process was painful for all involved. Nevertheless, the research strategy was at least partially successful, for it helped to explain why the projects were in trouble. However, the insights came too late to do more than point out the mistakes that had already been committed.

NOTES

1. I wish to acknowledge my appreciation to Irma Honigmann for her encouragement and editorial assistance in revising this paper.

2. "Failure" is being defined here in terms of the goals cited in the project proposal, which were twofold: improvement of beef and of the Masai level of living. Failure is not so clear-cut in the Masai project at present since, at last word, it has not formally ended. However, if this "failure" is not turned into "success," again using proposal criteria, then Masai culture may in the long run be destroyed since many of the material improvements are helping the non-Masai cultivators and not the Masai cattle-herders.

3. In fact, one of the agricultural technicians was so convinced that I was unnecessary and anyone could do my job that he tried to come up with sociological conclusions based on some interviews he conducted. These were put into an appendix of the published report (Passey, Hamilton, et al. 1969).

REFERENCES

Barnett, H. G., 1956. *Anthropology in Administration* (Evanston, Ill.: Row Peterson).

Foster, G. M., 1962. *Traditional Cultures: And the Impact of Technological Change* (New York: Harper and Row).

———, 1969. *Applied Anthropology* (Boston: Little, Brown).

Goodenough, W. H., 1962. The Growing Demand for Behavioral Science in Government: Its Implications for Anthropology. *Human Organization* 21:172–176.

Hamilton, J. W., 1969. Problems of Agricultural and Social Development Among the Kuria of Tanzania. (Manuscript.)

———, 1971. Masai Project Problems. (Manuscript.)

Orlans, H., 1968. Making Social Research More Useful to Government. *Social Science Information* 7(6):151–158.

Passey, A. J., and J. W. Hamilton, et al., 1969. *Tanzania: Land Use and Agricultural Diversification* (Washington, D.C., United States Department of Agriculture).

Pelto, P. J., 1970. *Anthropological Research: The Structure of Inquiry* (New York: Harper and Row).

The Contributors

Wilfrid C. Bailey is professor of anthropology and head of the Department of Anthropology at the University of Georgia, Athens. His major interests have been in community studies, change and development, and the anthropology of education.

Cora S. Balmat is associate professor in the School of Nursing at the University of Southern Mississippi, Hattiesburg. She is also project director under an NIMH grant for "Mental Health Concept Integration in the Baccalaureate Nursing Program."

George R. Fischer is a research archeologist with the National Park Service's Southeast Archeological Center in Tallahassee, Florida, where he is involved in the research programs of areas of the National Park System within the Southeast. His major research interest is in underwater archeology, a field in which he has investigated submerged sites in Arizona, Florida, and Texas.

Jeffrey B. Freeland is staff anthropologist at the NIMH Clinical Research Center at Lexington, Kentucky. His primary interests are the contemporary cultures of North America, rural and urban, indigenous and immigrant. His research has included studies of the economic integration of Indians in a rural community and various aspects of narcotic addiction.

Carl M. Gussin is staff ethnographer for the Institute for Behavioral Research at Hyattsville, Maryland. His major interests are in anthropology and education. He has done field research in India, in Israel, and in an urban community in Wisconsin. He is primarily concerned with the question of change in response to external stimuli.

James W. Hamilton is associate professor of anthropology at the University of Missouri, Columbia. He has carried out research in Thailand and Tanzania on culture change in tribal cultures as they come into contact with the state. His major interests are social and economic organization, culture change and evolution, method and theory in social anthropology.

James Hawkins is director of education of the Bureau of Indian Affairs, Washington, D.C., with an interest in comparative educational systems among minority and dependent peoples.

William R. Maples is associate professor of anthropology at the University of Florida, Gainesville. He is a specialist in physical anthropology with research interests in primate biology and behavior, particularly of African monkeys.

Dan F. Morse is survey archeologist for the Arkansas Archeological Survey and associate professor of anthropology at the University of Arkansas, Jonesboro and at Arkansas State University, State University. He has worked extensively in the eastern United States and has published papers concerning most aspects of the prehistory of this region. His primary interests are Early Man, lithic technology, Shell Mound Archaic, Illinois Hopewell, and the development of the Mississippi stage in the Mississippi Valley.

Alden Redfield is director of the Museum of Anthropology and an instructor in the Department of Anthropology at the University of Missouri, Columbia. His major fields are archeology (early man studies in North America) and museology (research and development of museum techniques). He has done field work in Mexico, Yugoslavia, and Luxembourg.

C. Ronald Rosenstiel is staff anthropologist at the NIMH Clinical Research Center at Lexington, Kentucky, and is currently working on a Ph.D. dissertation in applied anthropology at the University of Kentucky. His research to date has focused on some of the problems related to disaster relief, domestic and recreational water use, and drug abuse.

Stephen L. Schensul is director of community research for the Community Mental Health Program at the Illinois State Psychiatric Institute, Chicago. He is also assistant professor in the Department of Anthropology at the University of Illinois, Chicago Circle, as well as in the Department of Psychiatry at the University of Illinois at the Medical Center, Chicago. He has conducted field research in northern Minnesota rural communities and among the Banyankole in Southwest Uganda. (The other members of the Community Research team who contributed significantly to the ideas in his paper are: Philip Ayala, Mary Bakszysz, Santiago Boiton, Kay Guzder, Alice Pizana, Emile Schepers, Elias Sevilla-Casas, Susan Stechnij, and their consultant Professor Pertti J. Pelto.)

Clyde C. Snow is chief of the Physical Anthropology Unit at the Federal Aviation Administration, Civil Aeromedical Institute, in Oklahoma City, Oklahoma. He also serves as a consultant in forensic anthropology to law enforcement agencies and medical examiners of Oklahoma and neighboring states. His research interests include aircraft accident investigation and improved methods of skeletal identification.

William C. Sturtevant is curator of North American anthropology at the Smithsonian Institution. Among his major interests are the ethnology of eastern North America and methods of research on material culture in the field and in museums.